Start with... A Heart

Draw Characters Using Heart Shapes

Created by STEVE HARPSTER

HARPTOONS™ PUBLISHING

www.harptoons.com

www.harptoons.com

Harpster, Steve
Start With A Heart - Draw Characters Using Heart Shapes
written and illustrated by Steve Harpster

SUMMARY: Learn how to draw characters starting with a heart shape
ART / General, JUVENILE FICTION / General

ISBN 13: 978-0-9995290-1-0
ISBN 10: 0-9995290-1-3

SAN: 859-6921

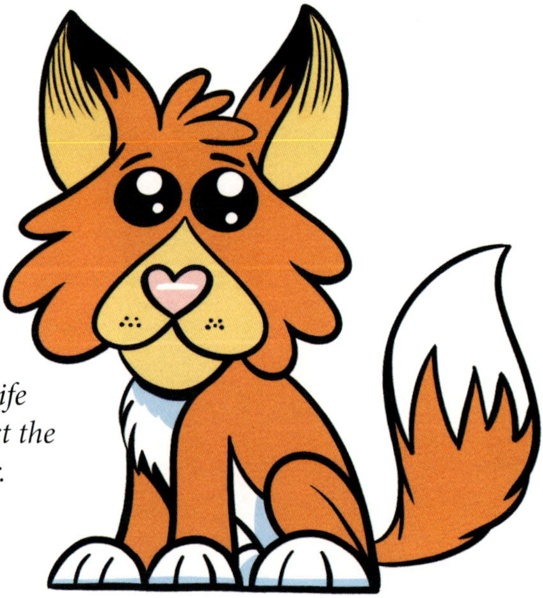

*To my amazing wife
who stole my heart the
moment I met her.*

Follow Harptoons on:

**For school visit information
www.harptoons.com or
contact Steve Harpster at
steve@harptoons.com**

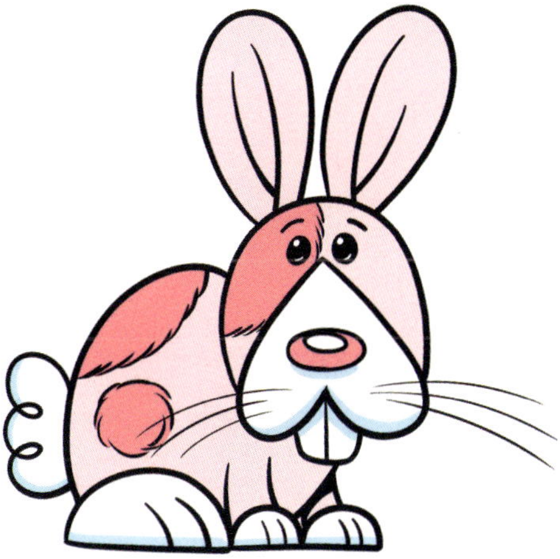

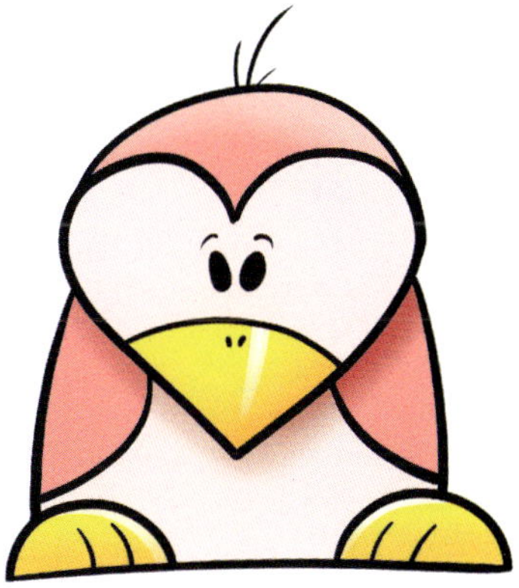

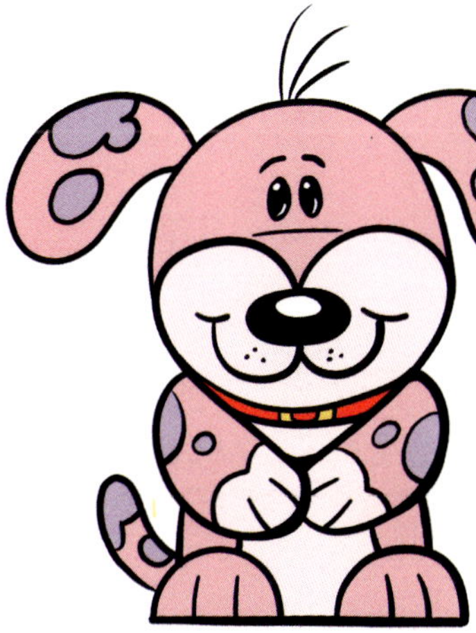

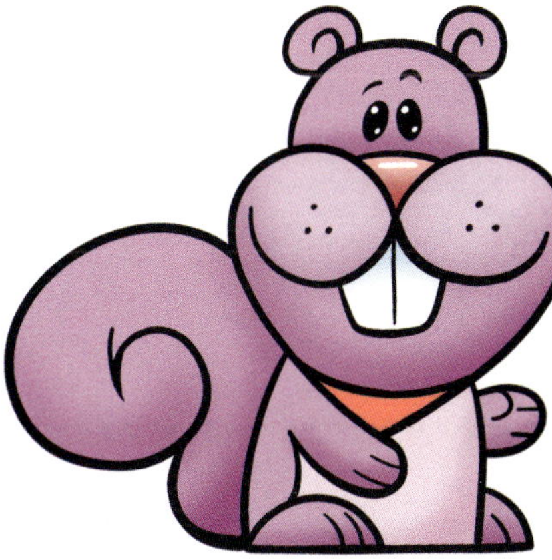

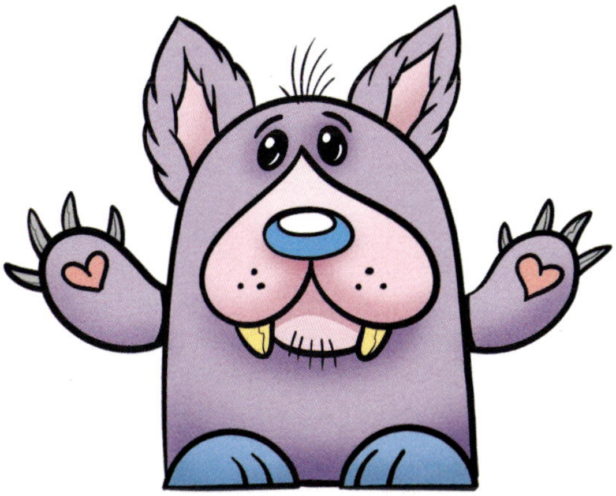

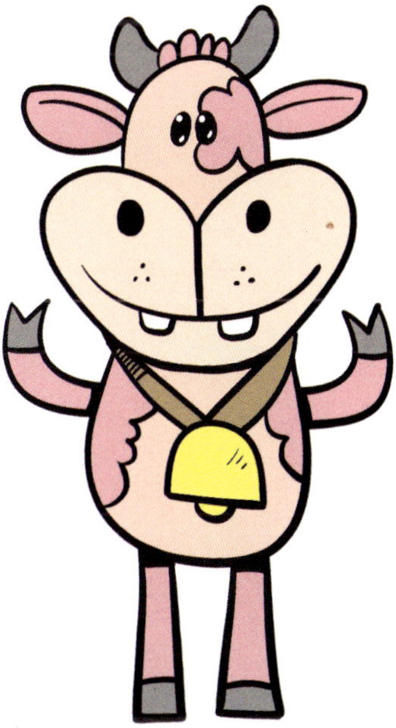

HEART STENCIL (FOR PERFECT HEARTS)

1. 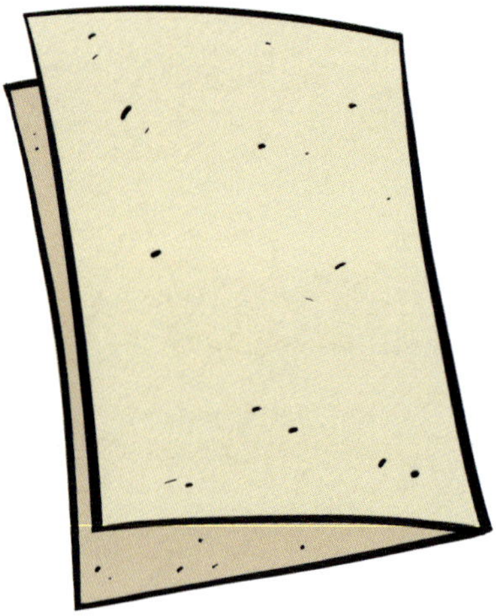

FOLD PAPER IN HALF

(HEAVY CARD STOCK WORKS BEST)

DRAW THIS SHAPE ON THE FOLDED EDGE

2. 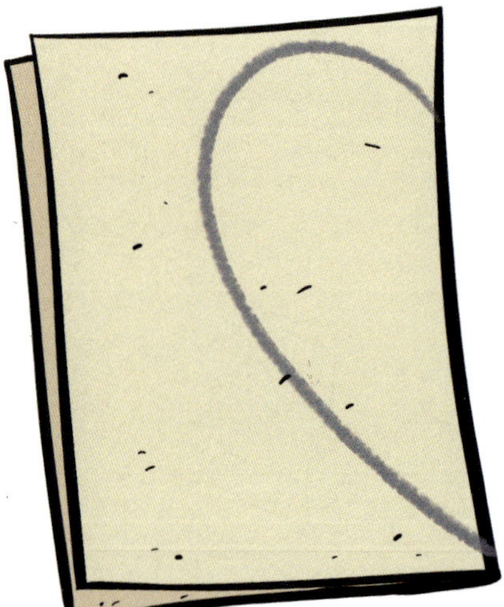

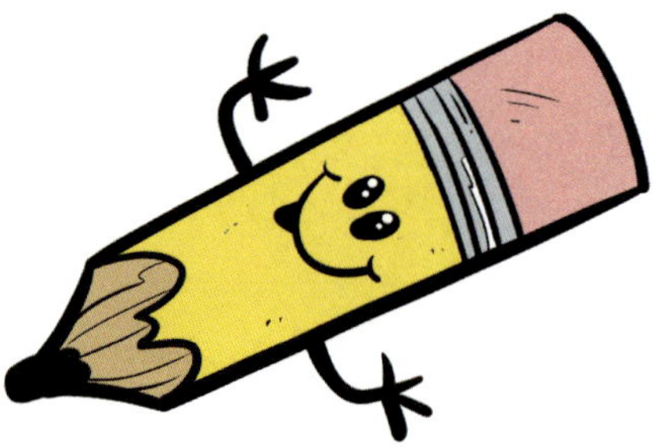

3. CUT OUT THE SHAPE

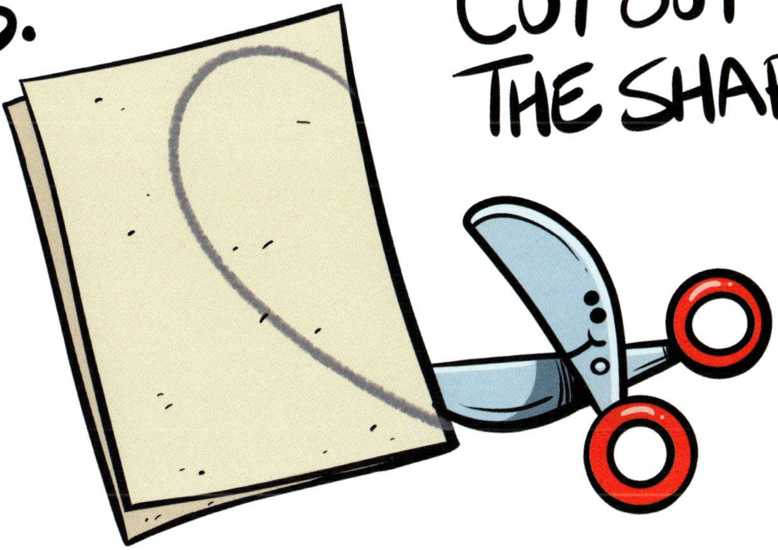

4. NOW YOU HAVE 2 HEART STENCILS

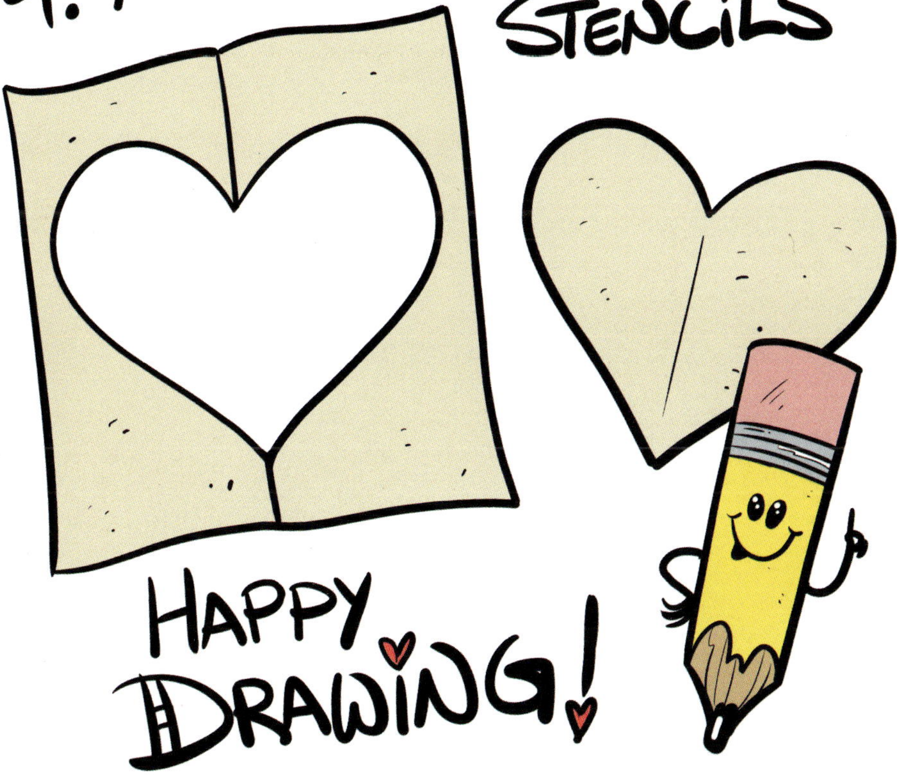

HAPPY DRAWING!

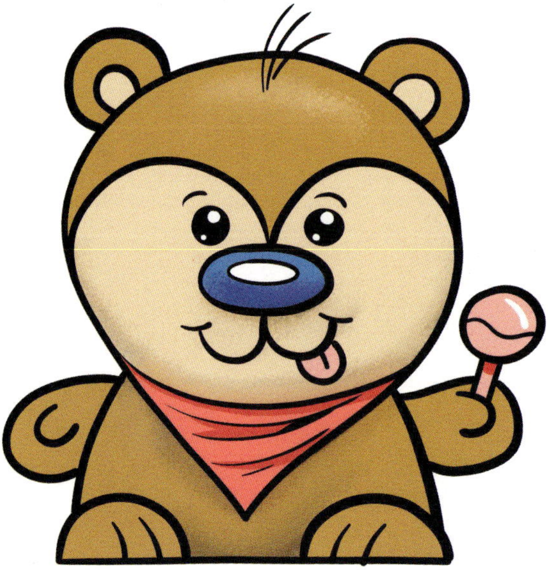

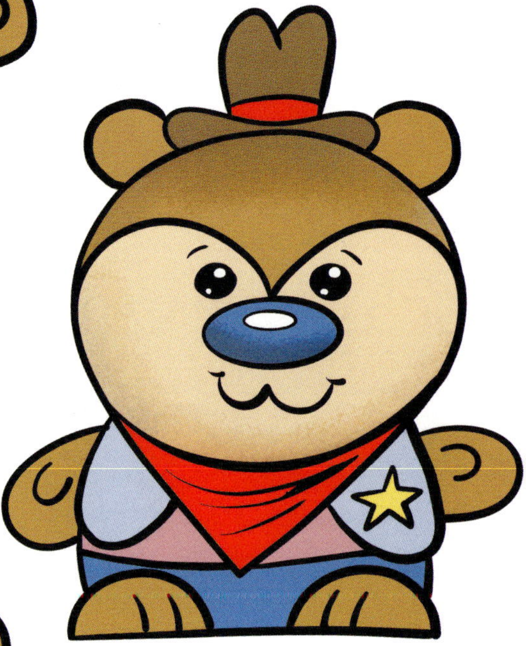

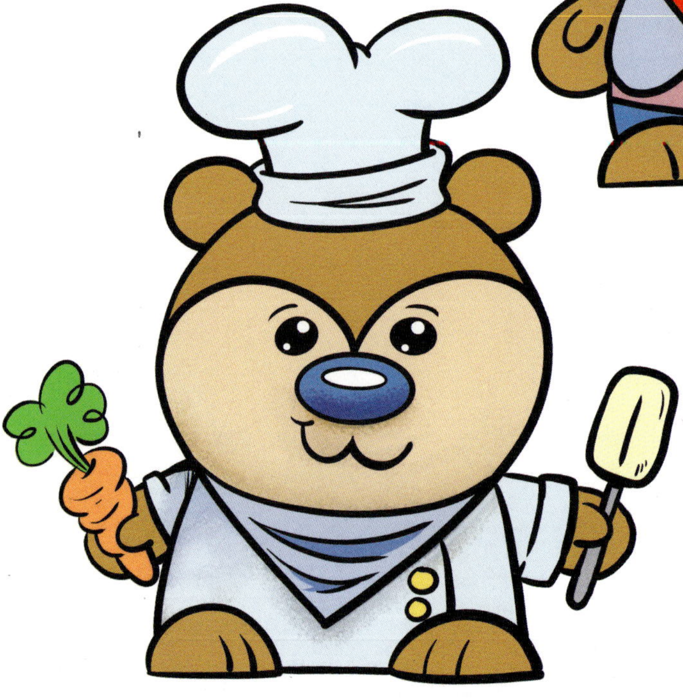

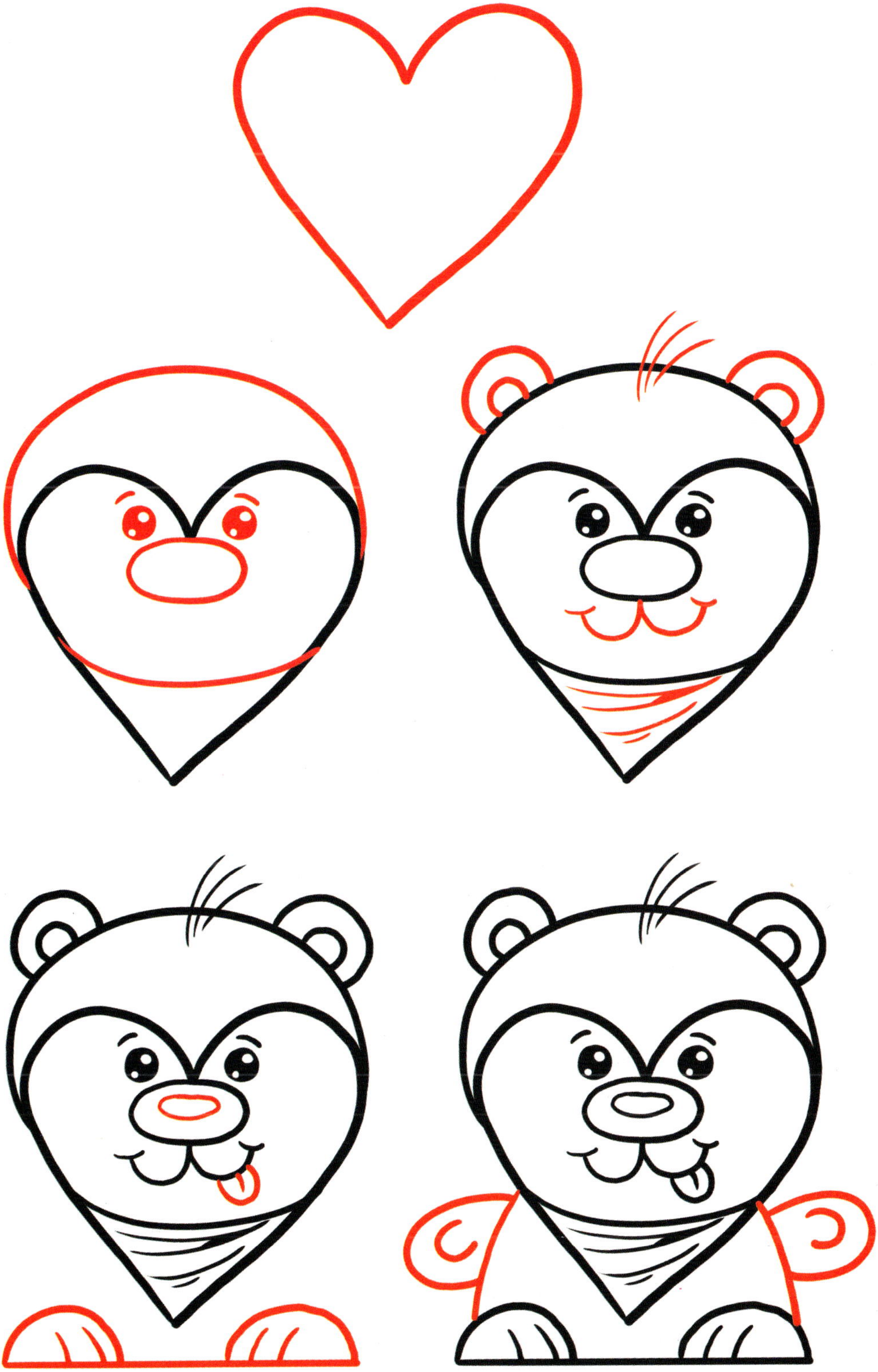

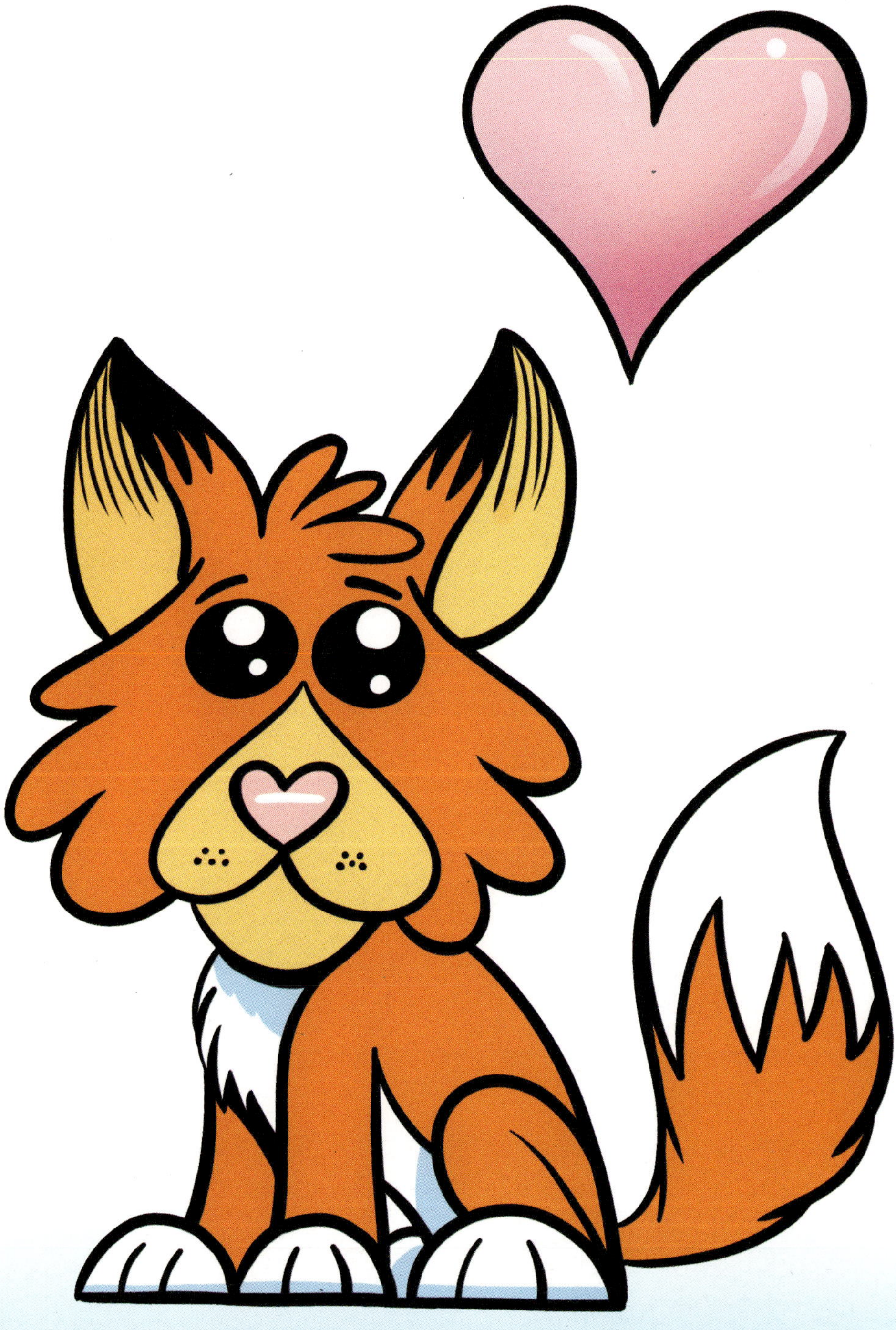

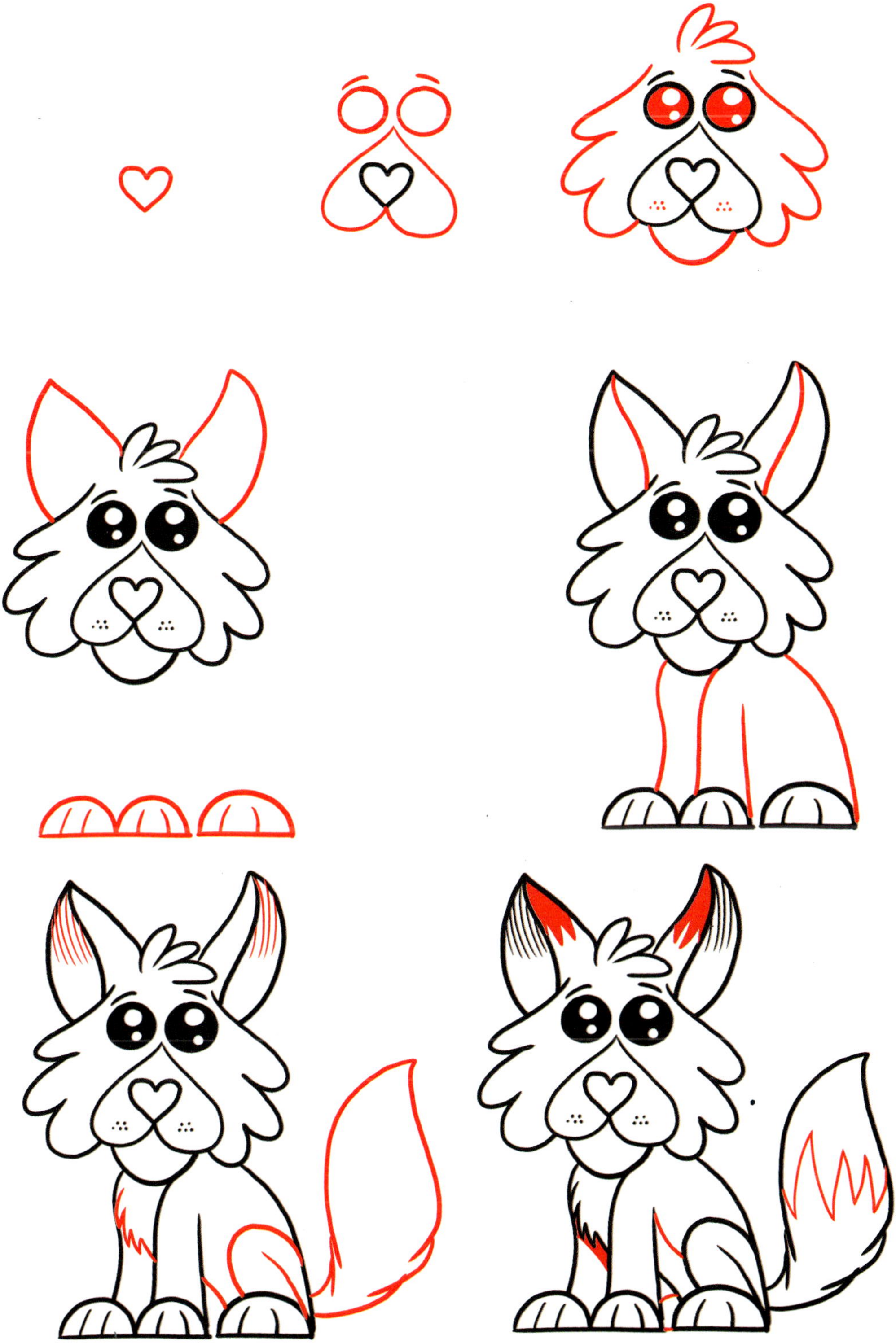

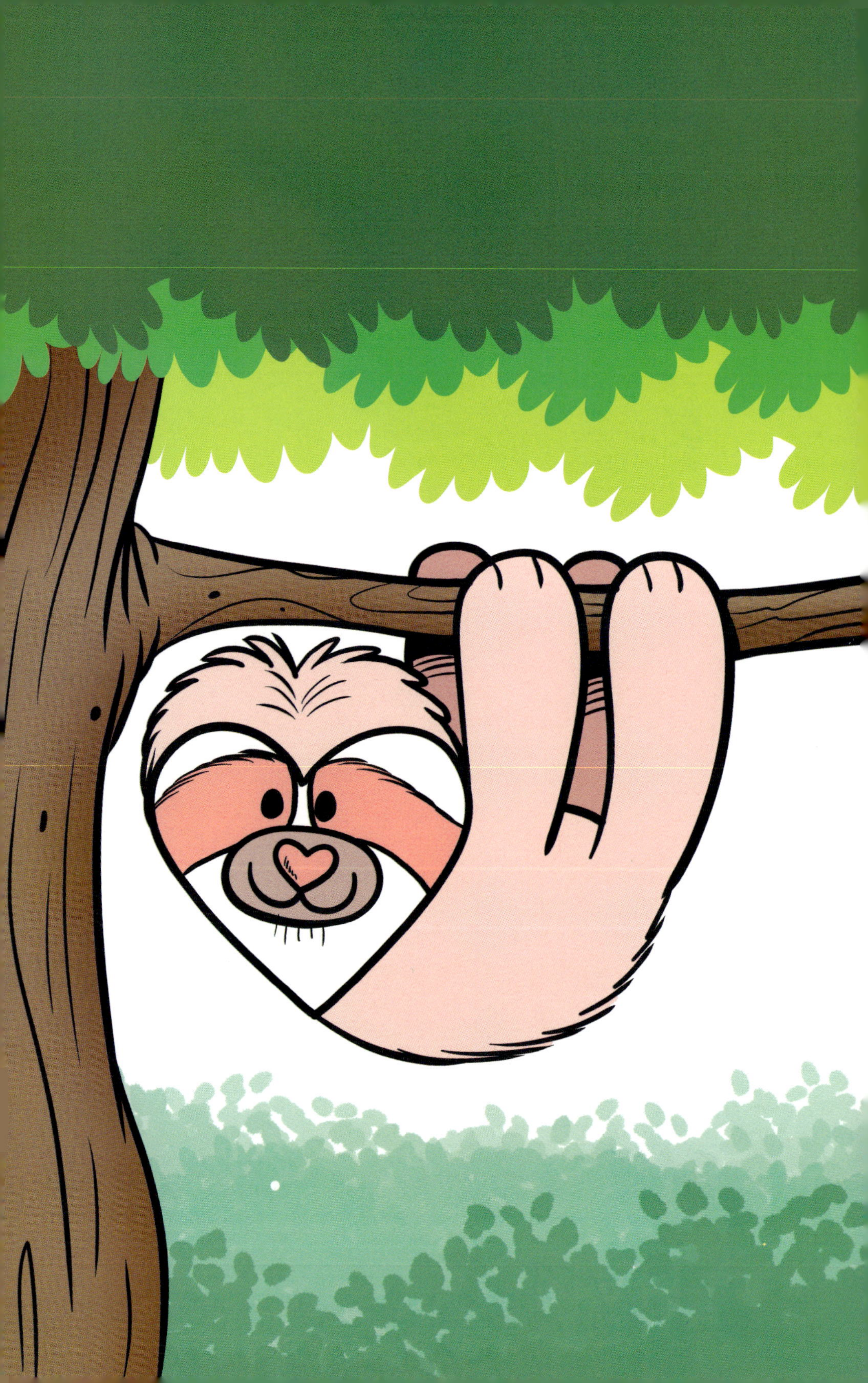

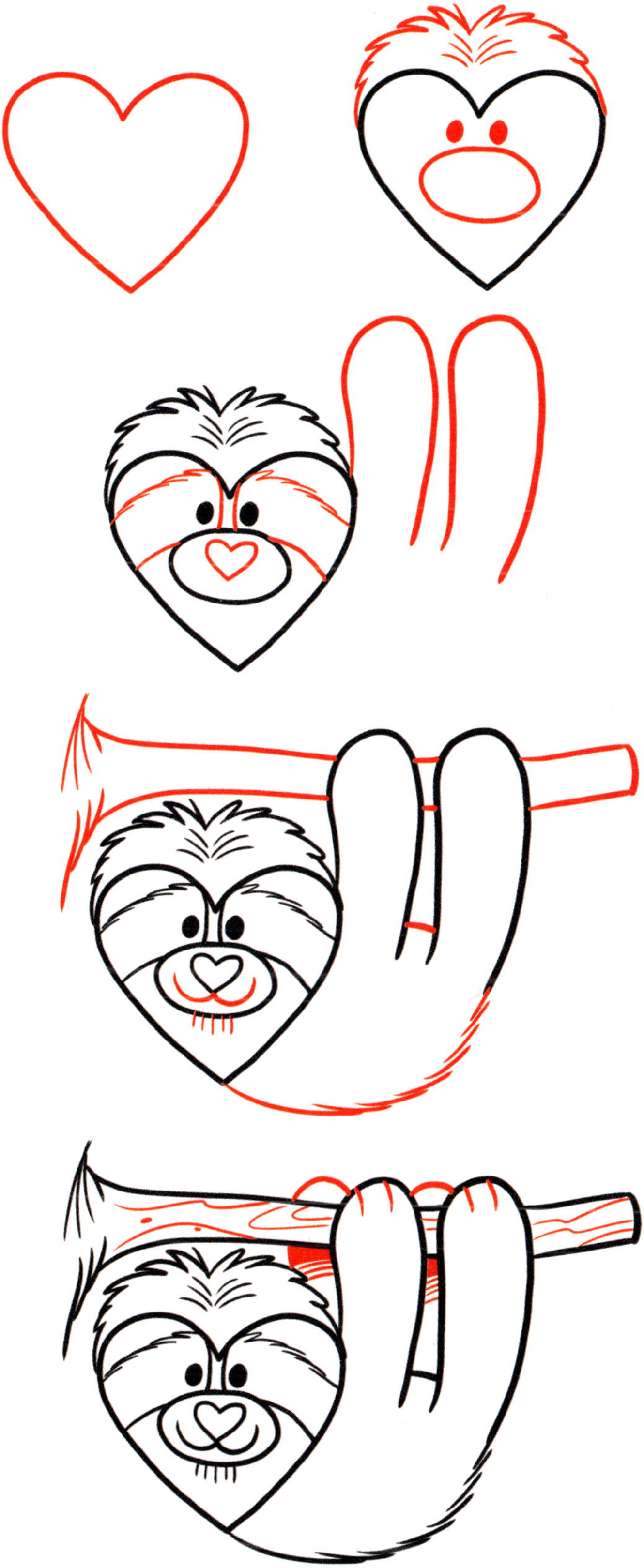

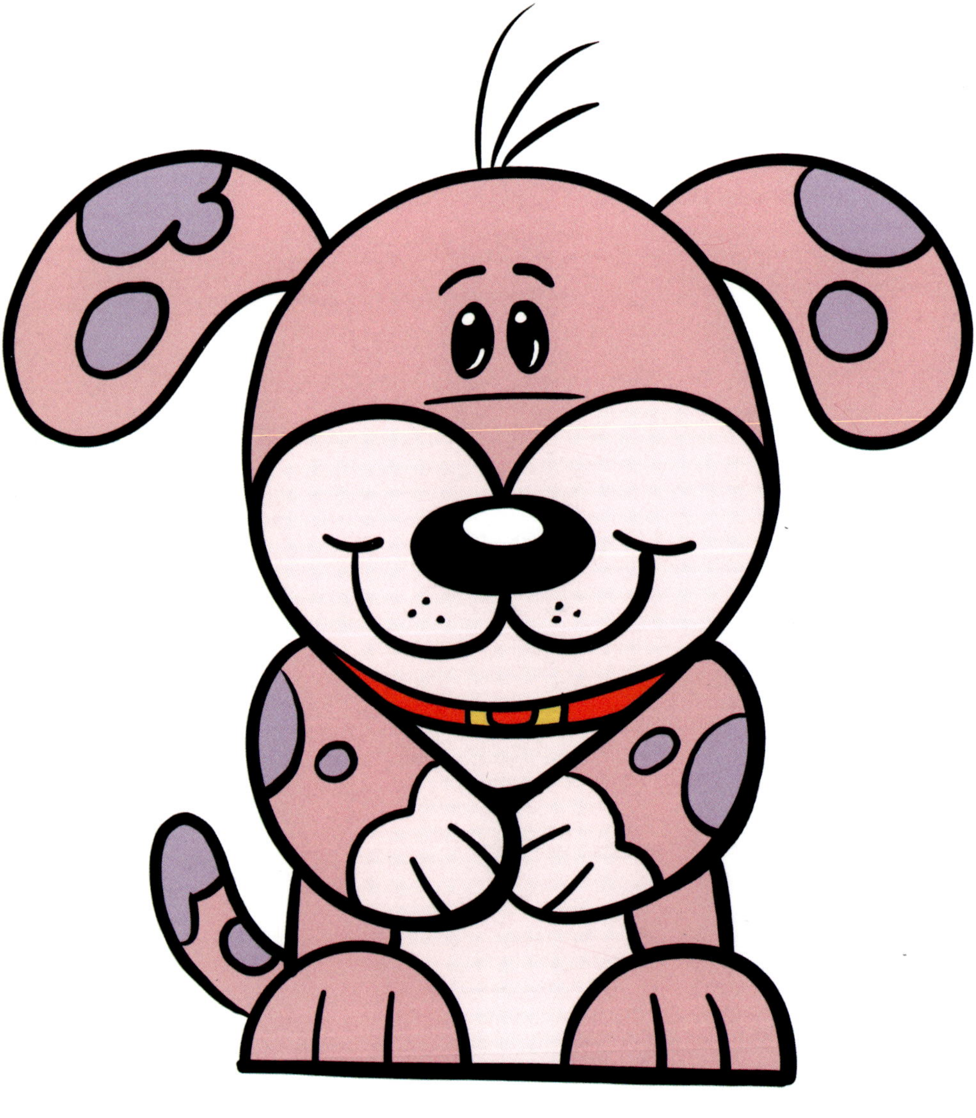

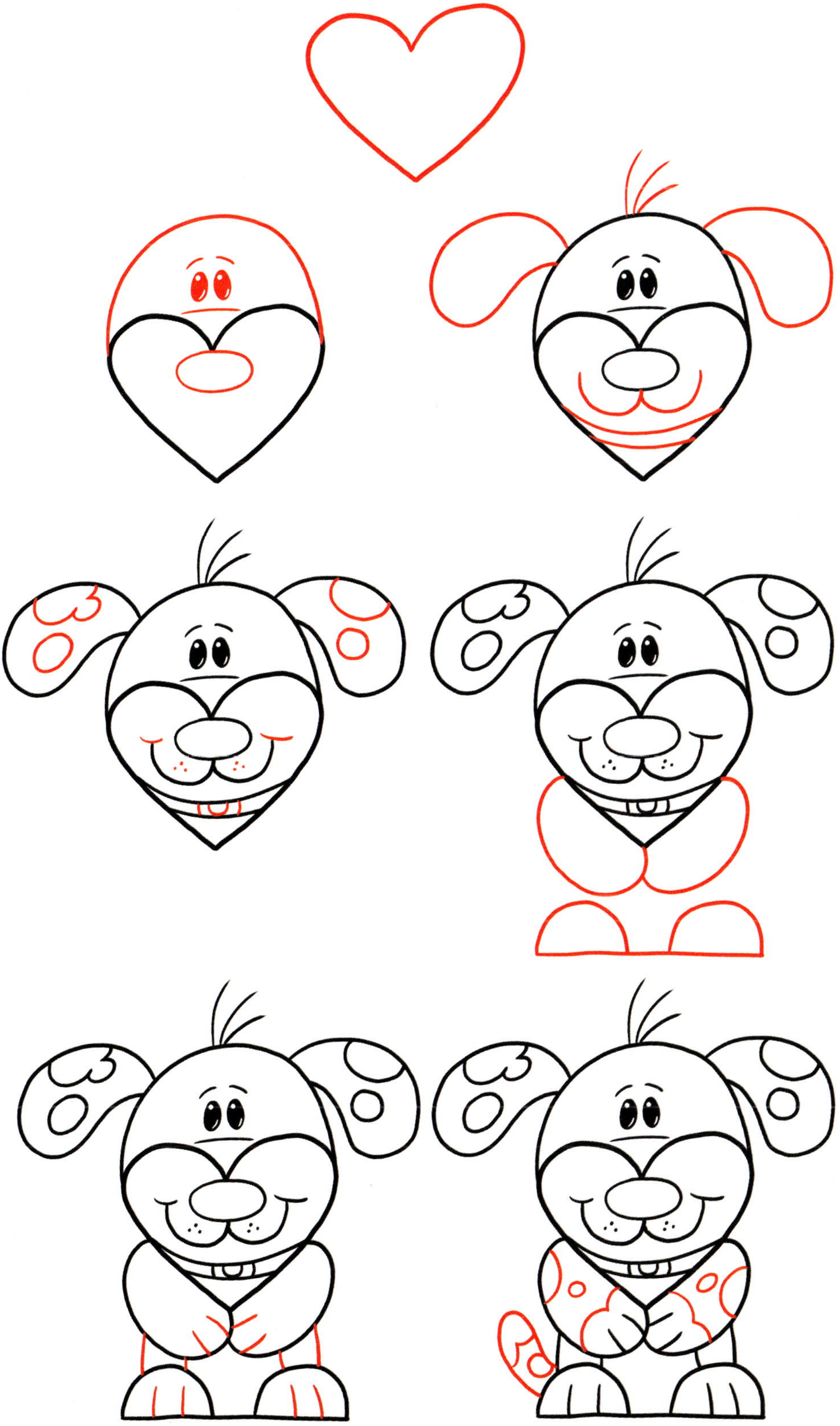

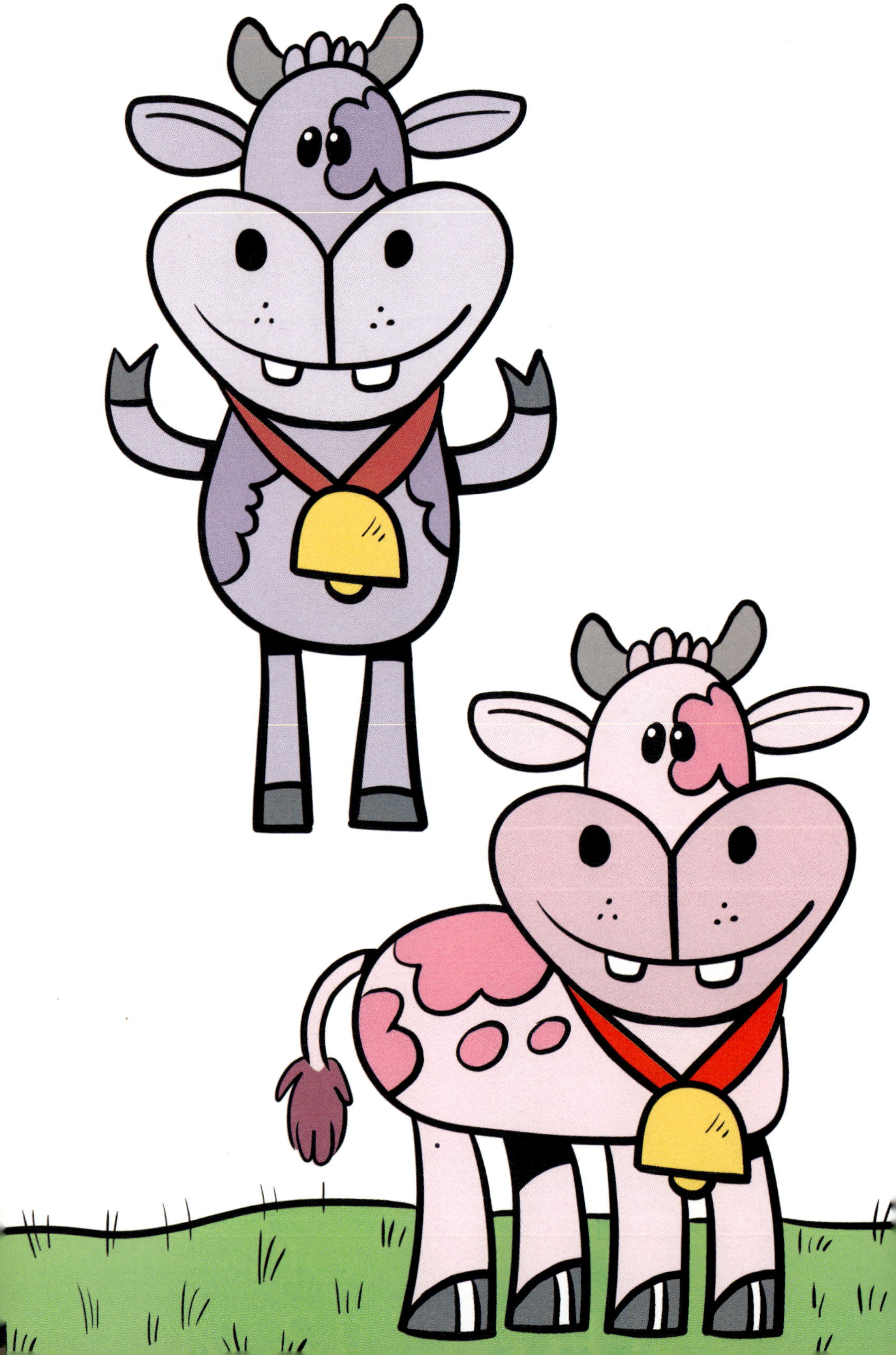

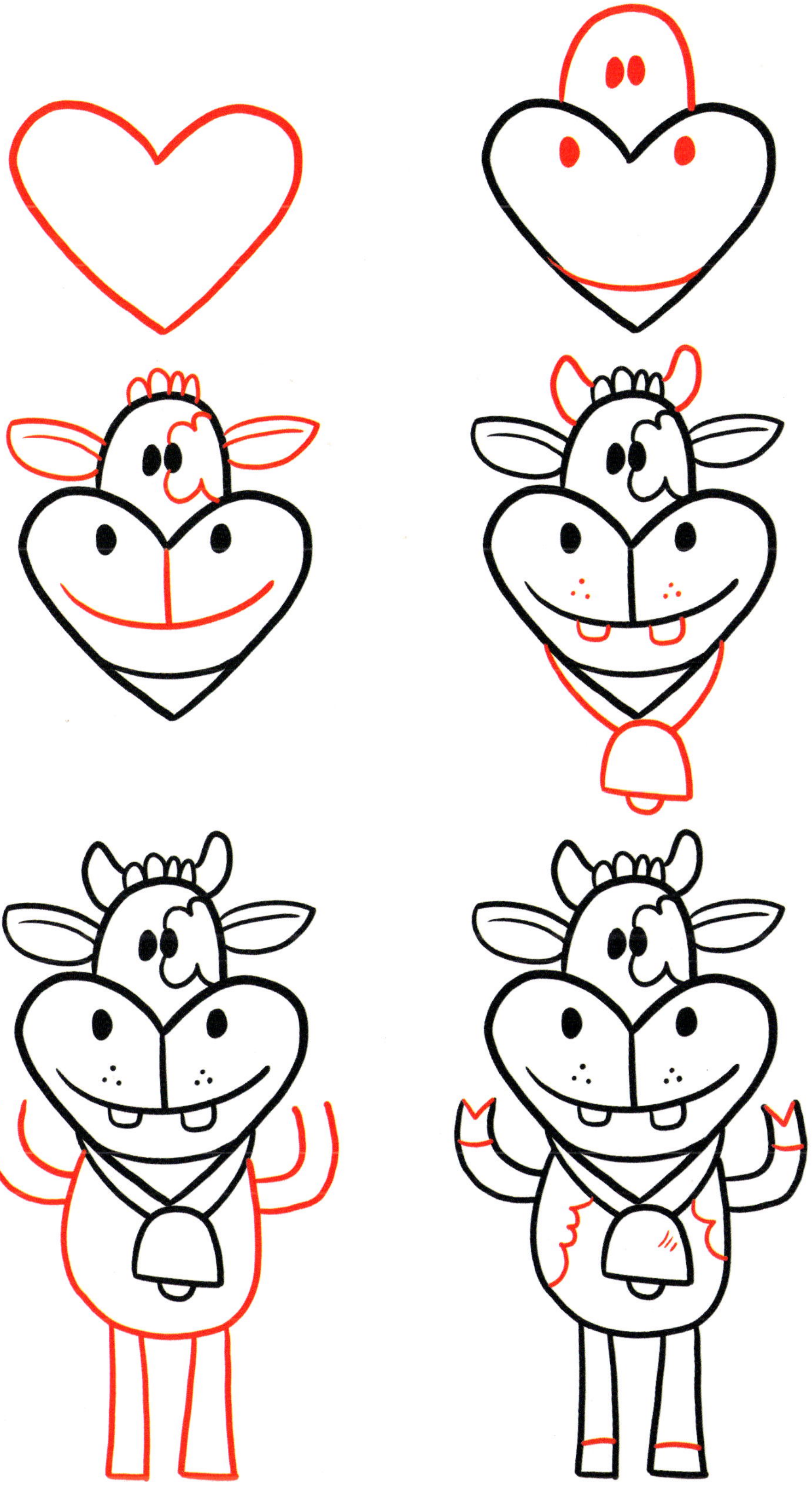

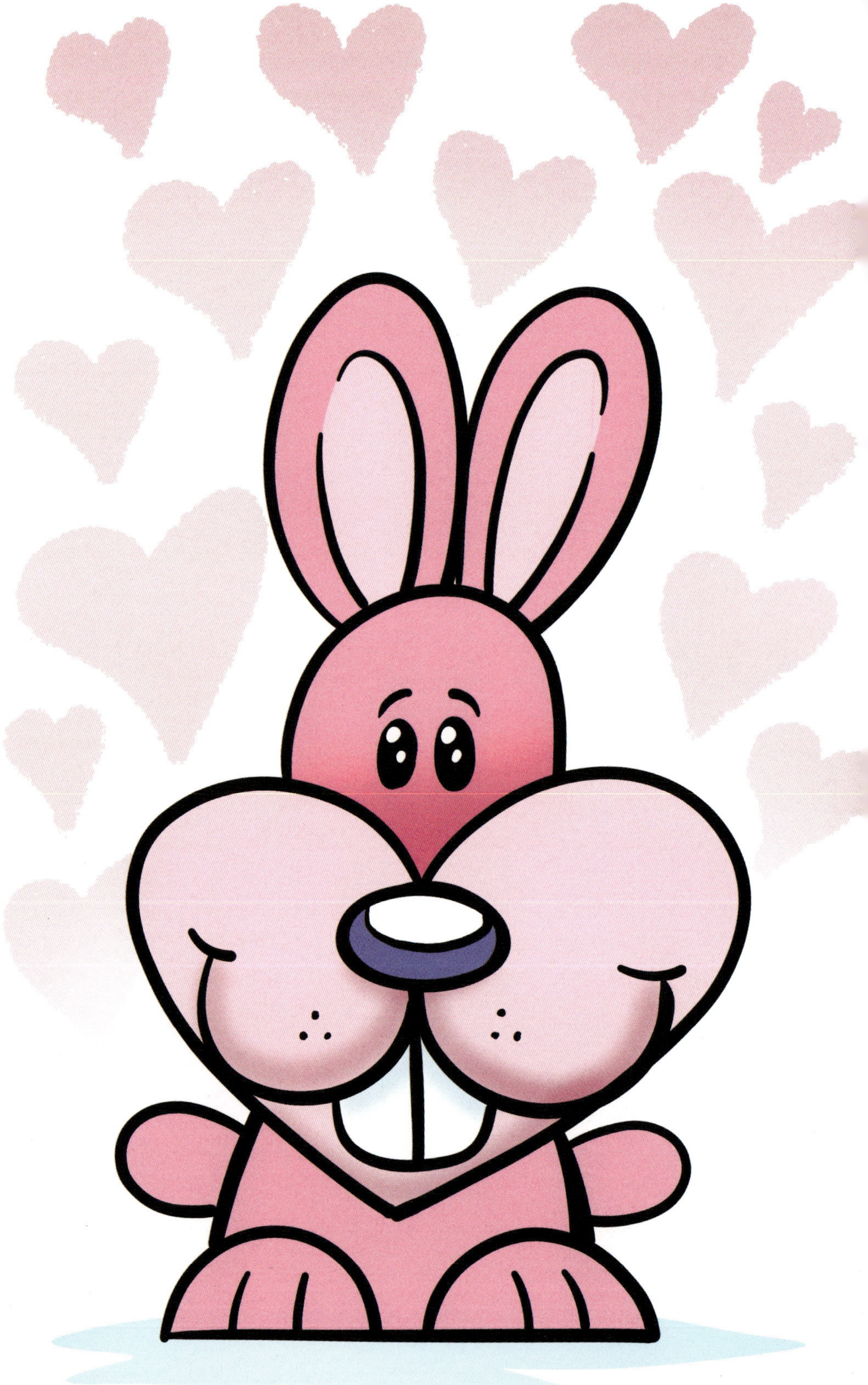

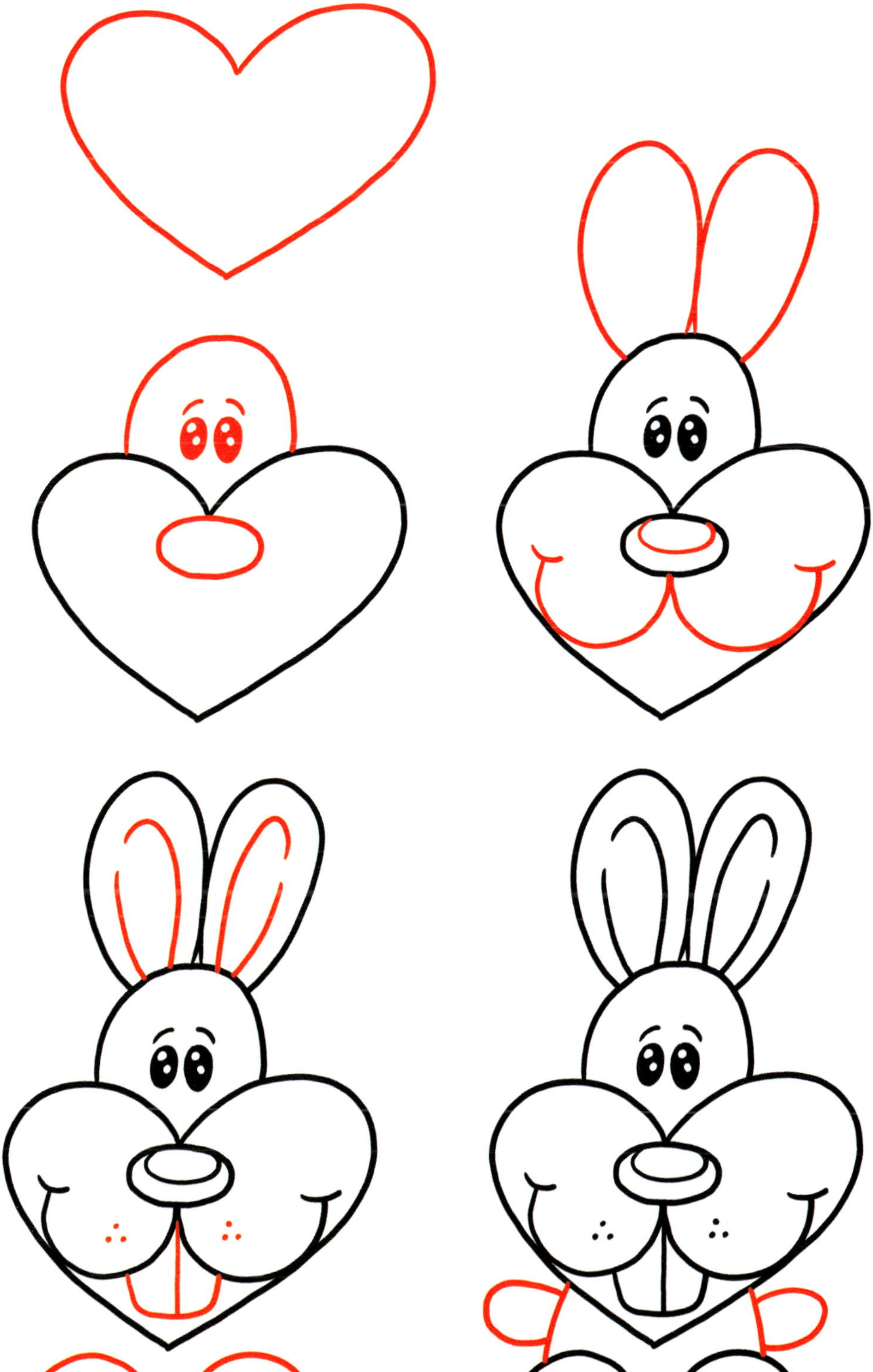

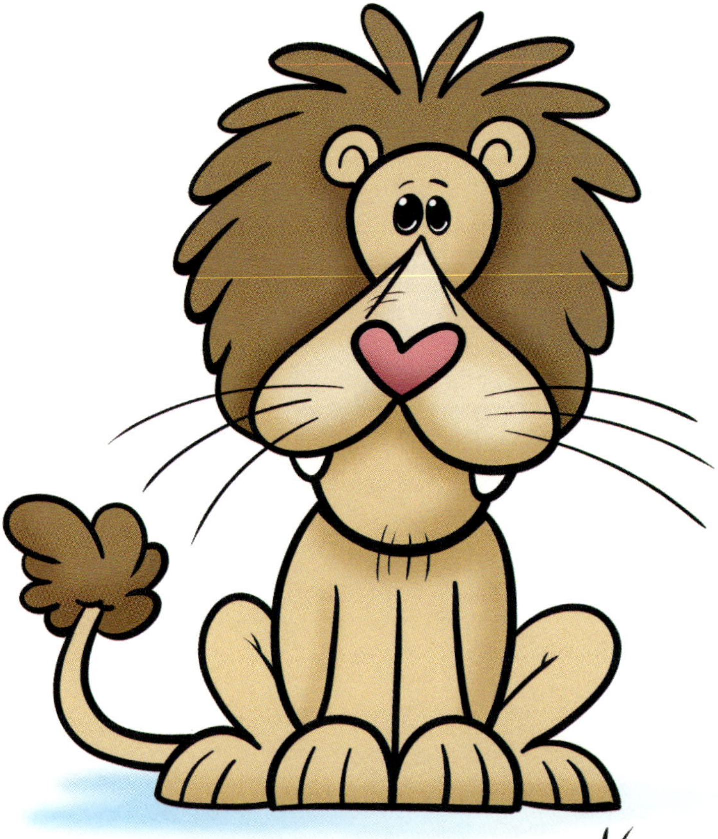

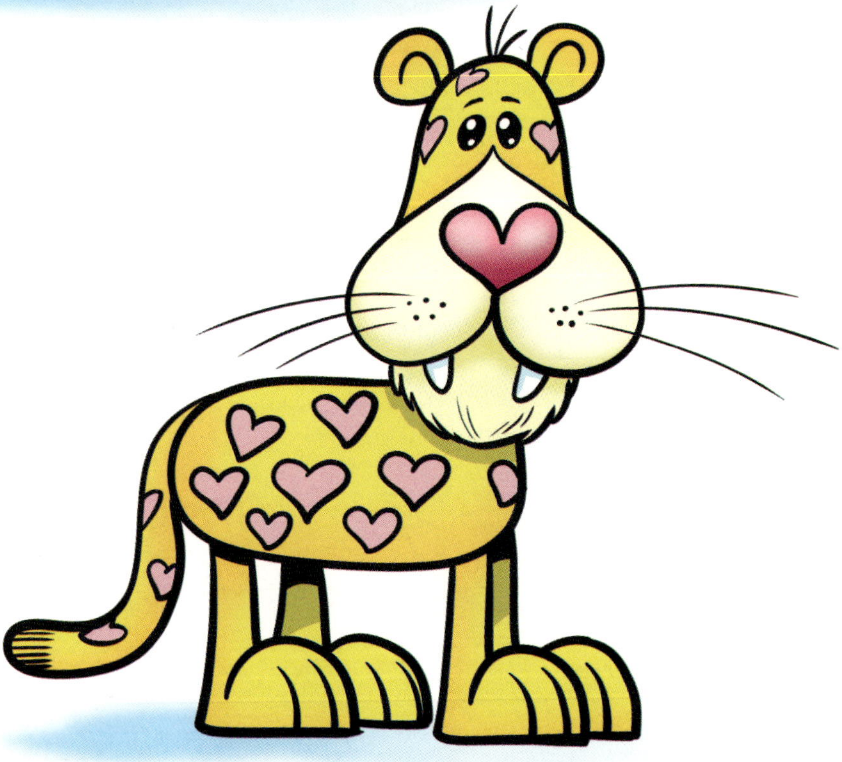

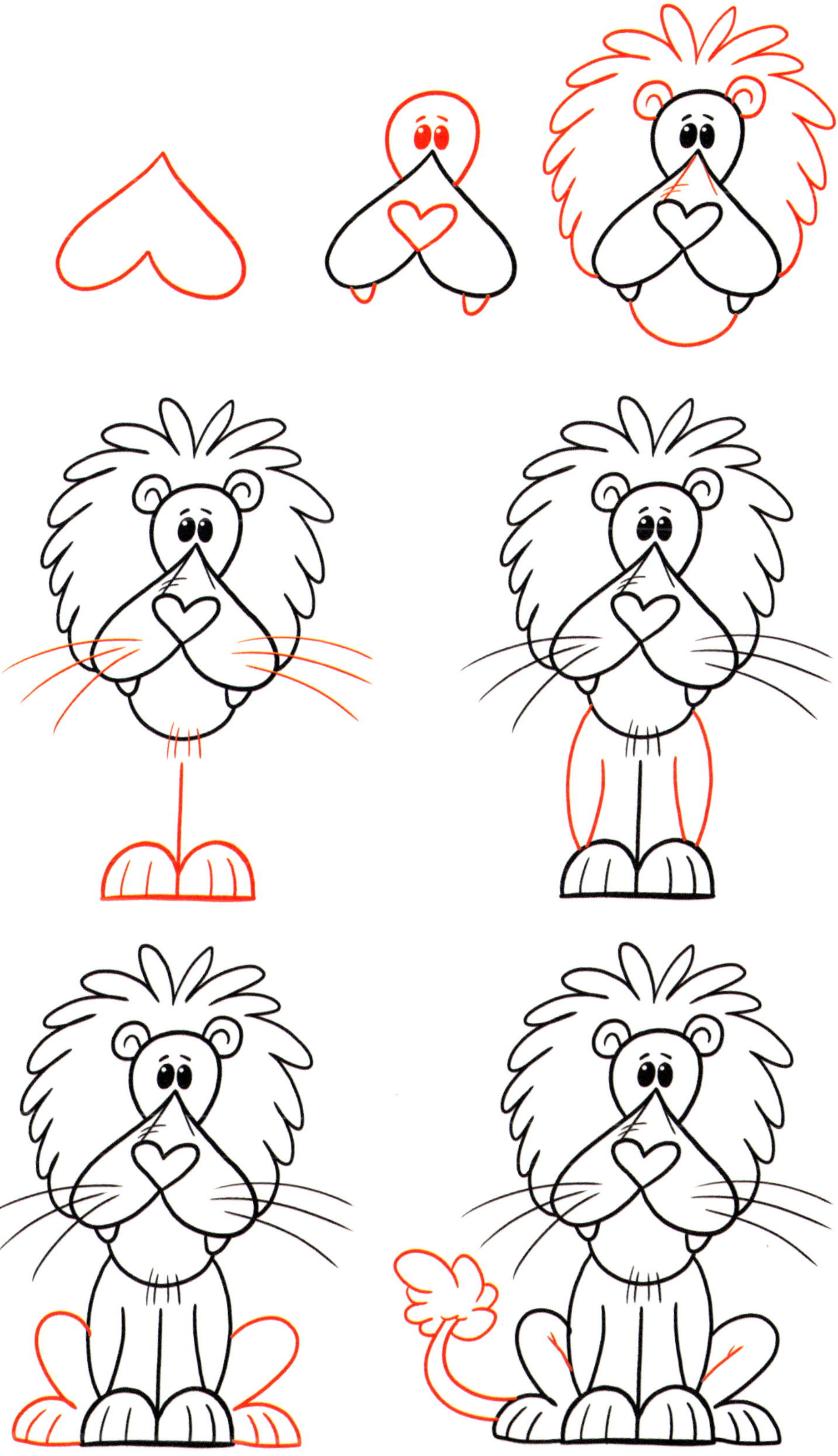

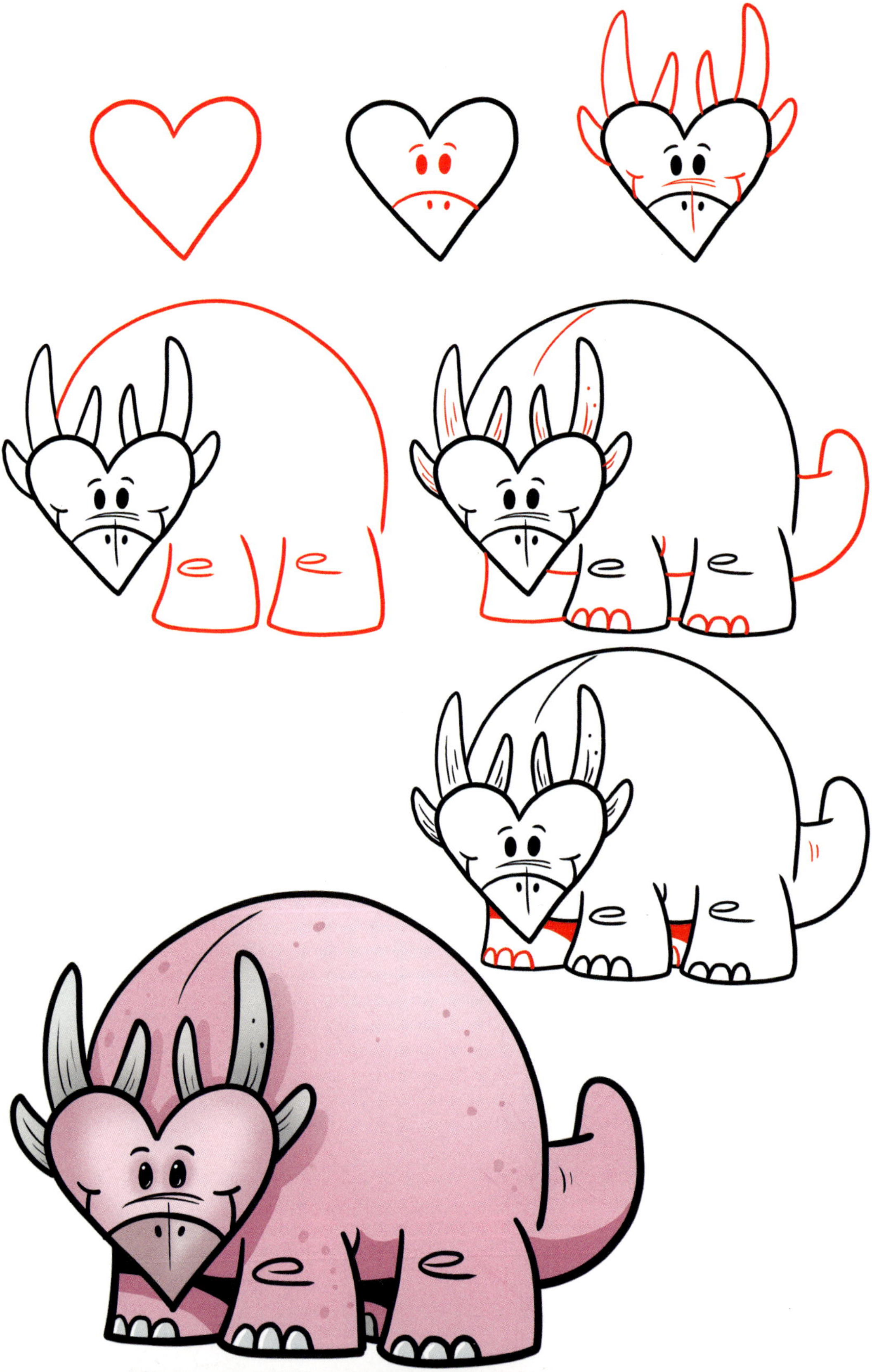

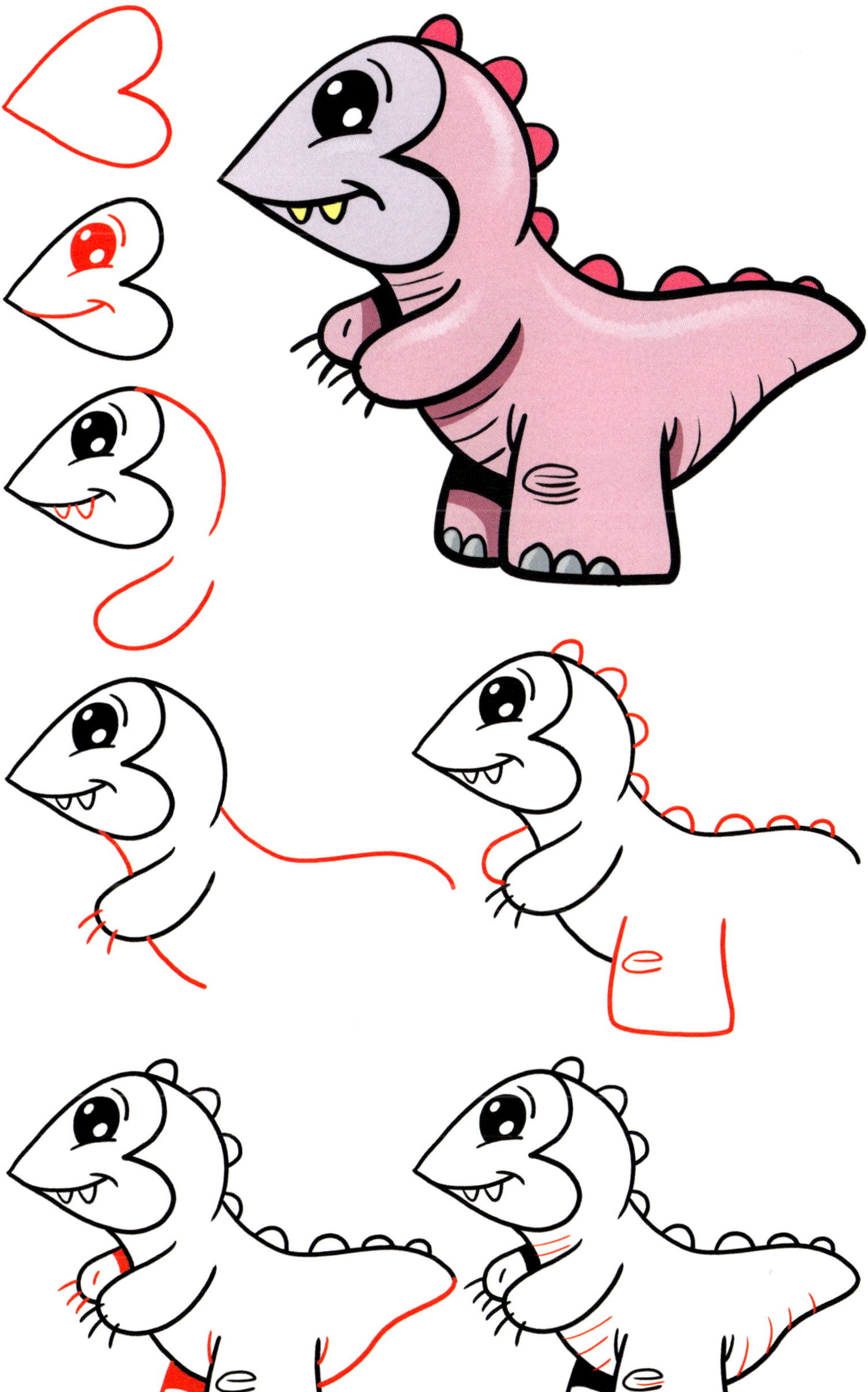

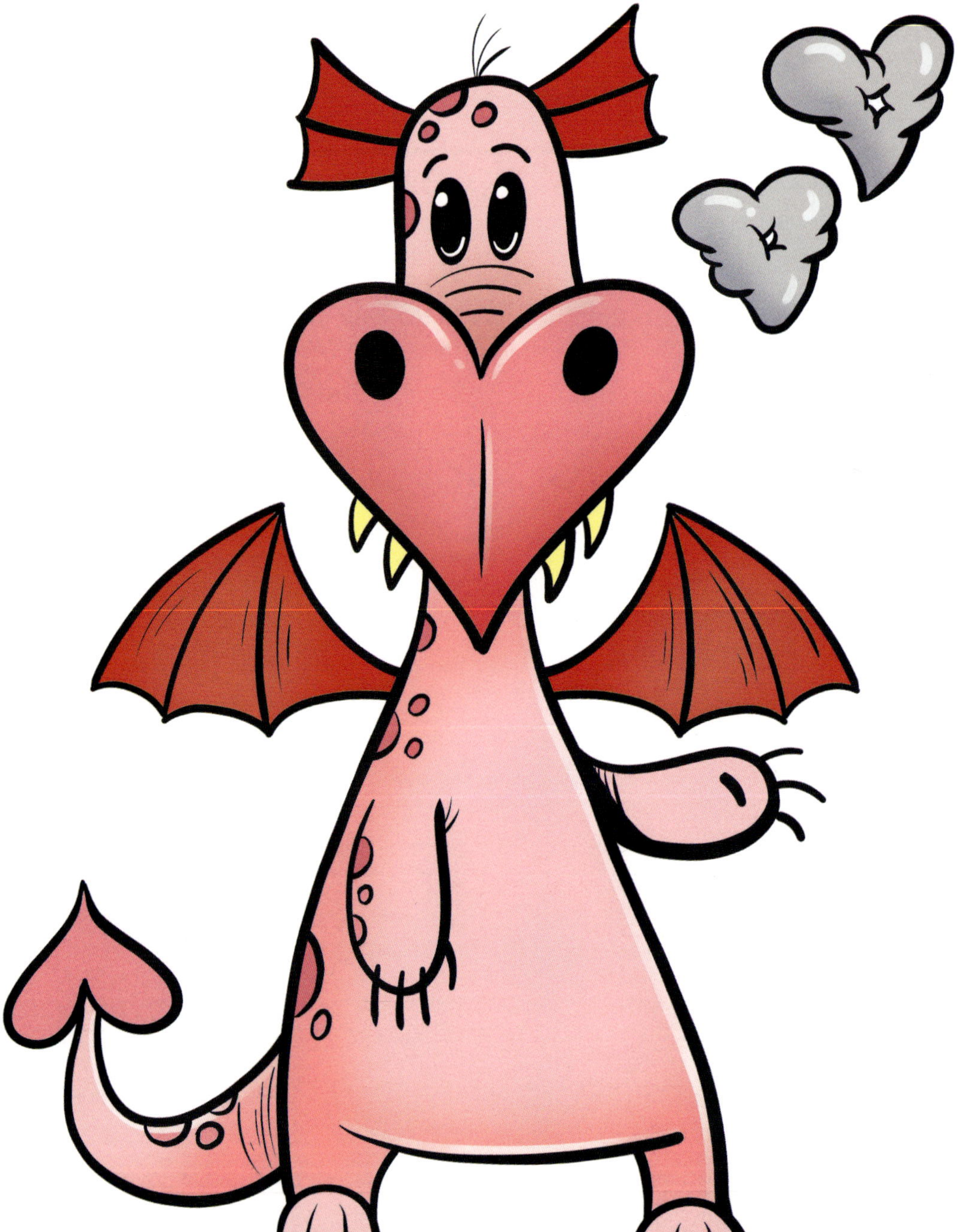

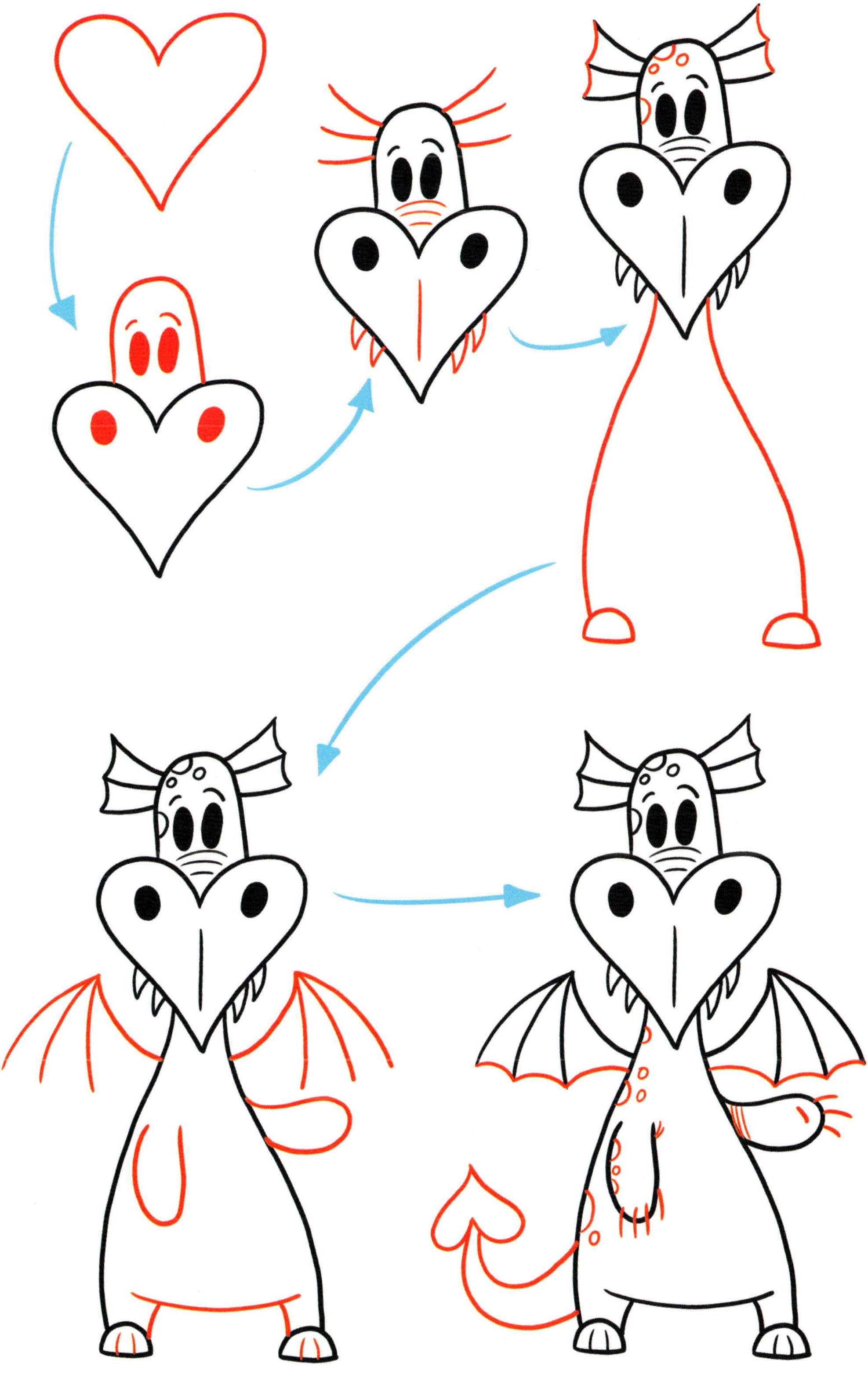

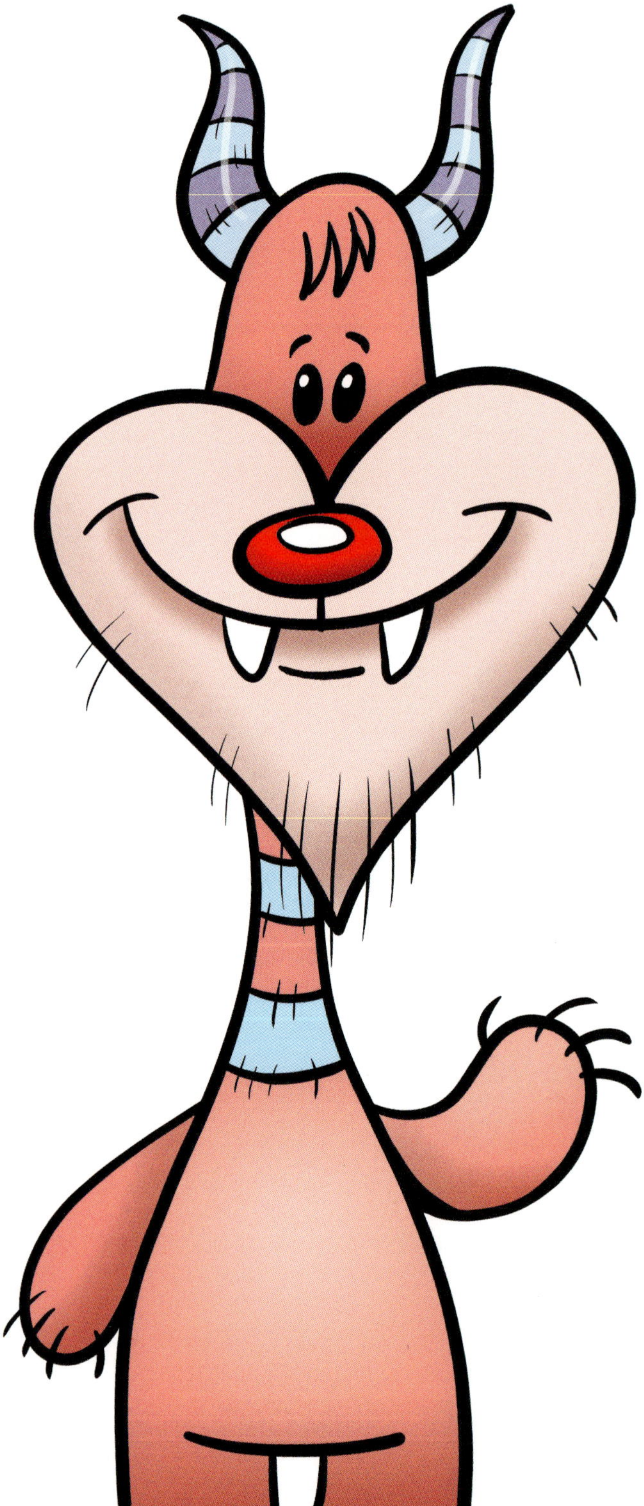

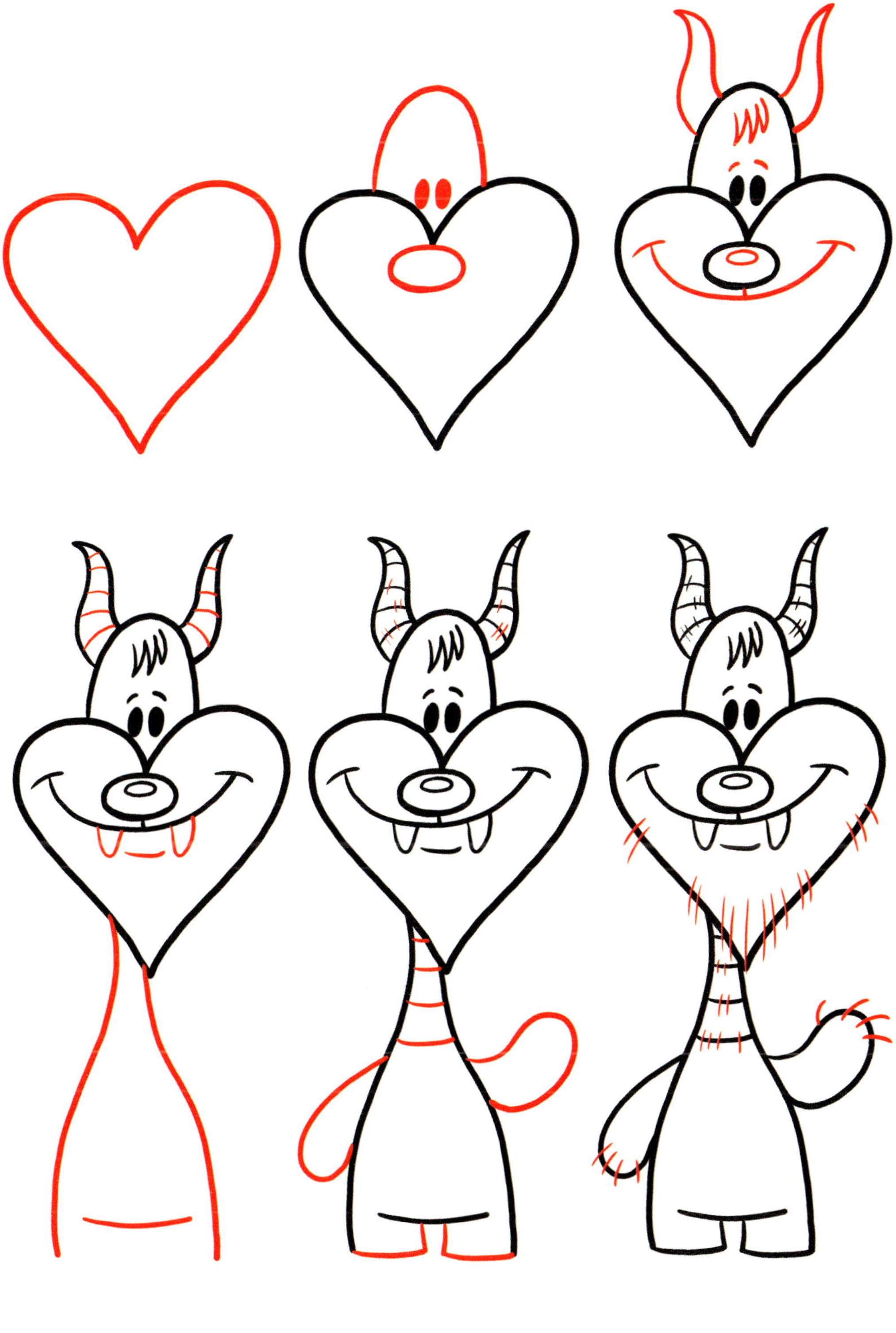

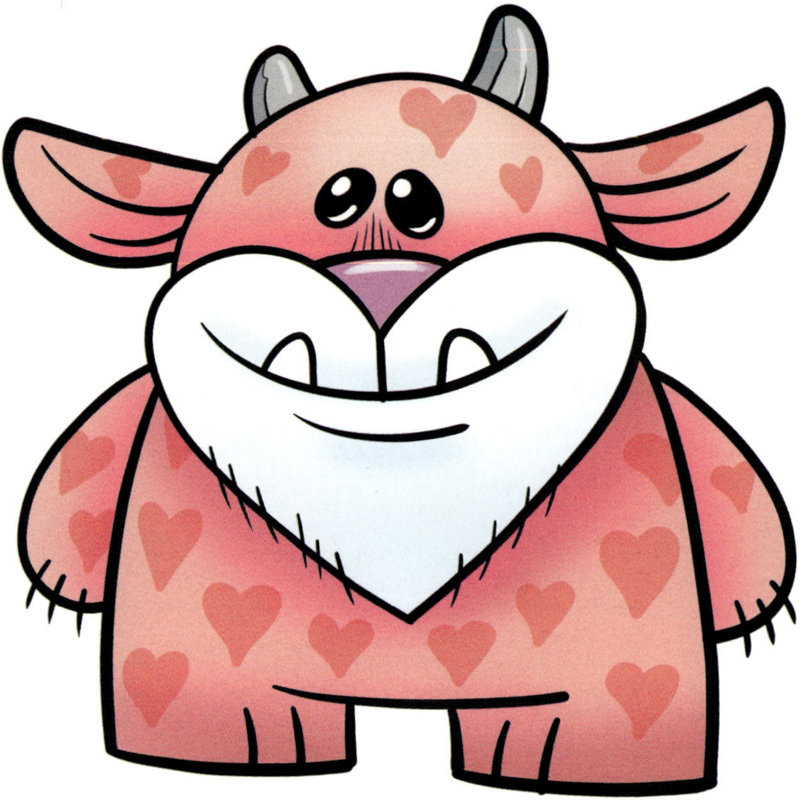

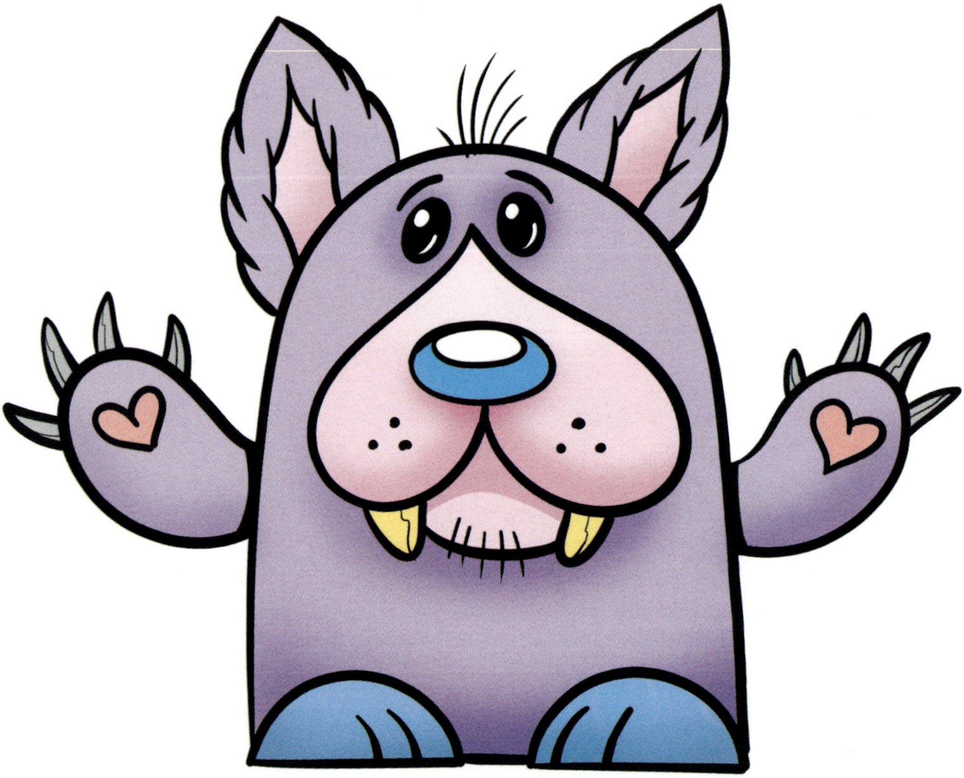

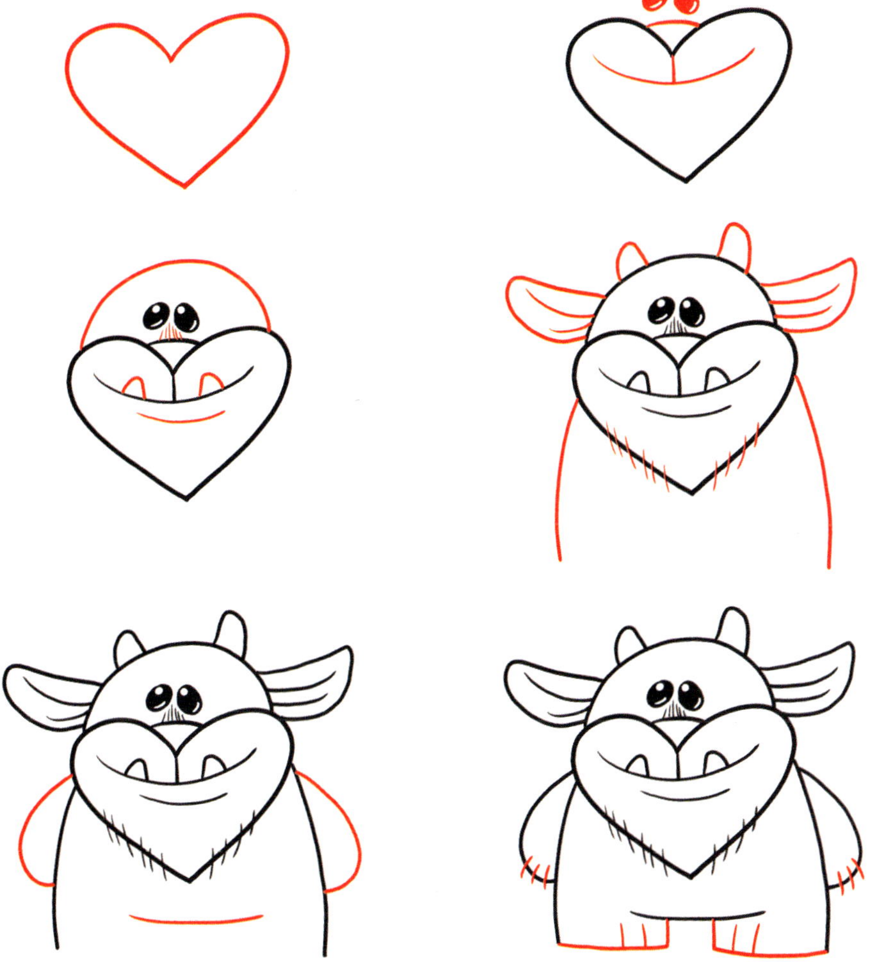

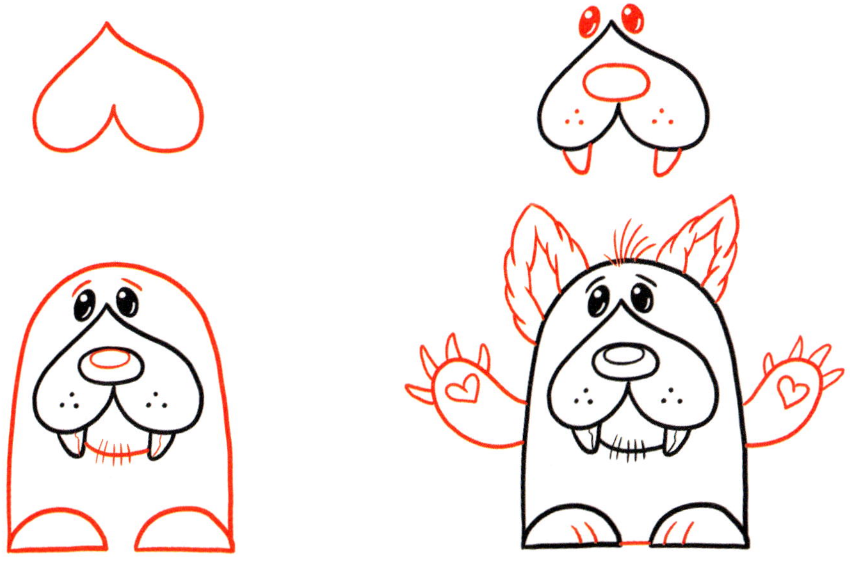

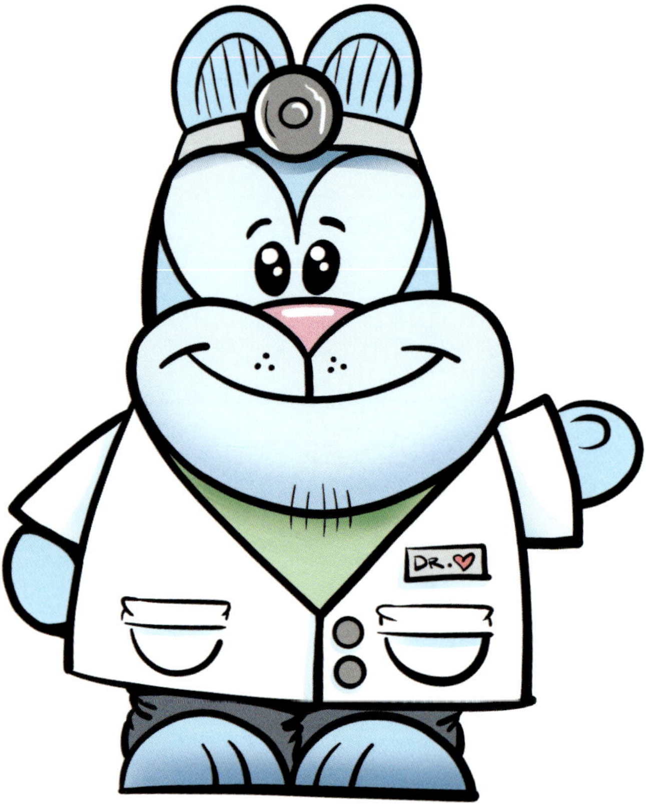
DR.

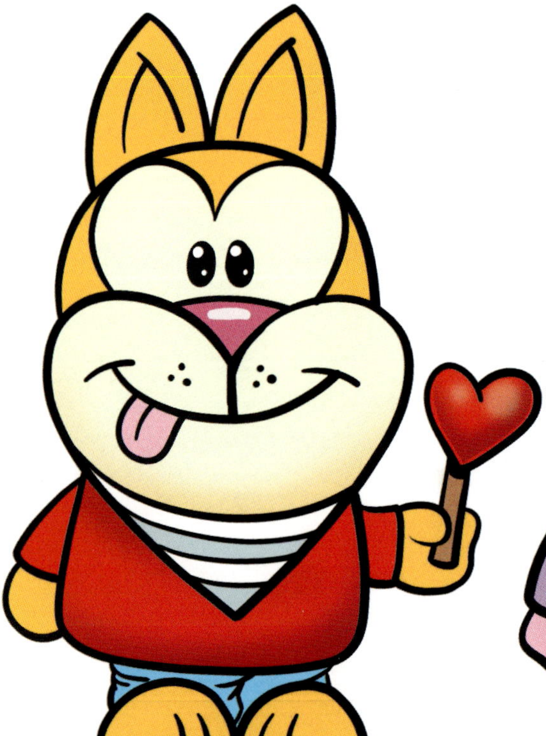

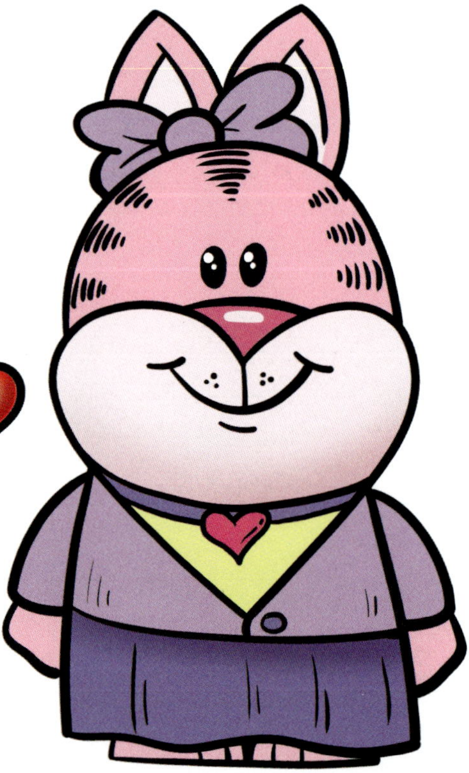

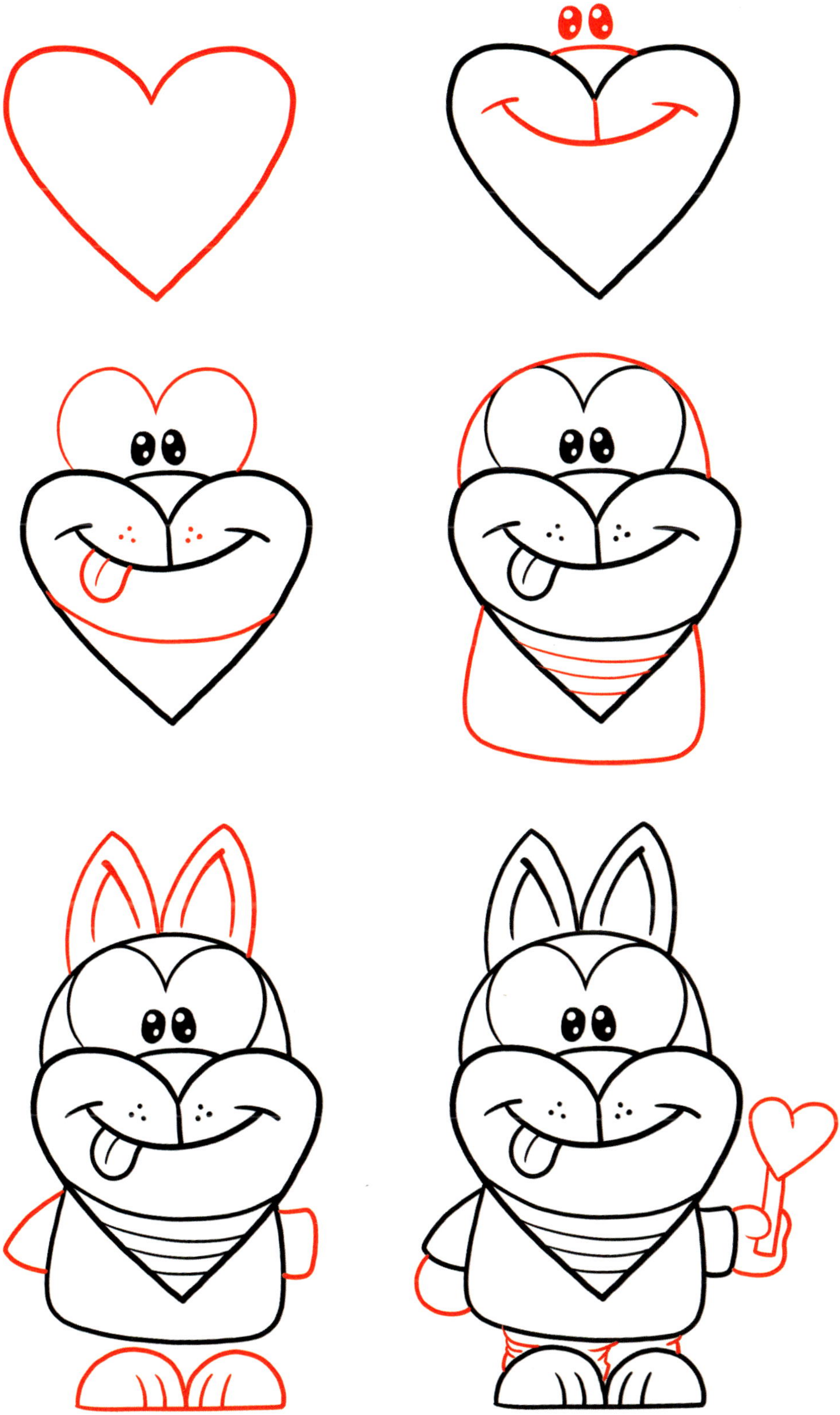

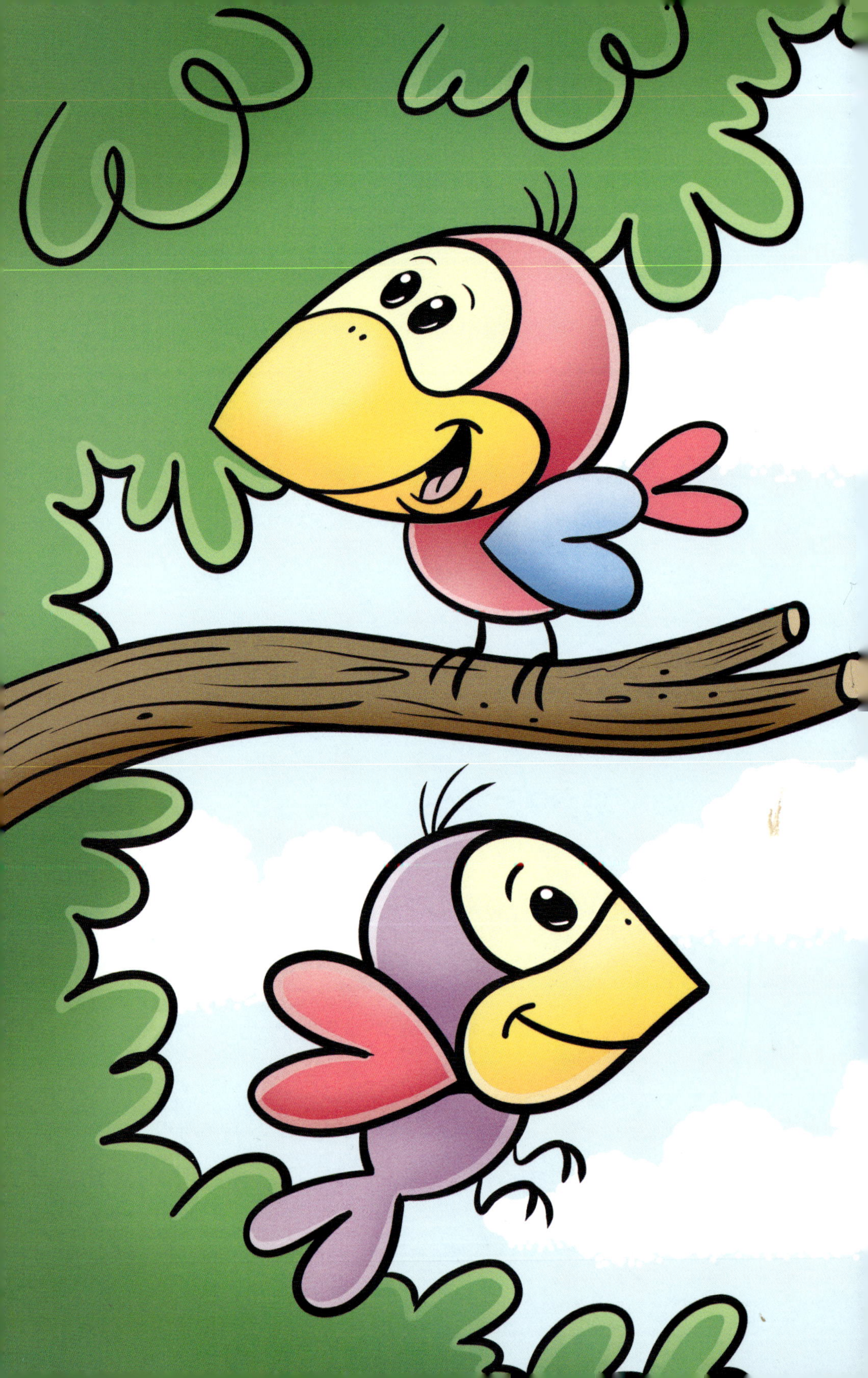

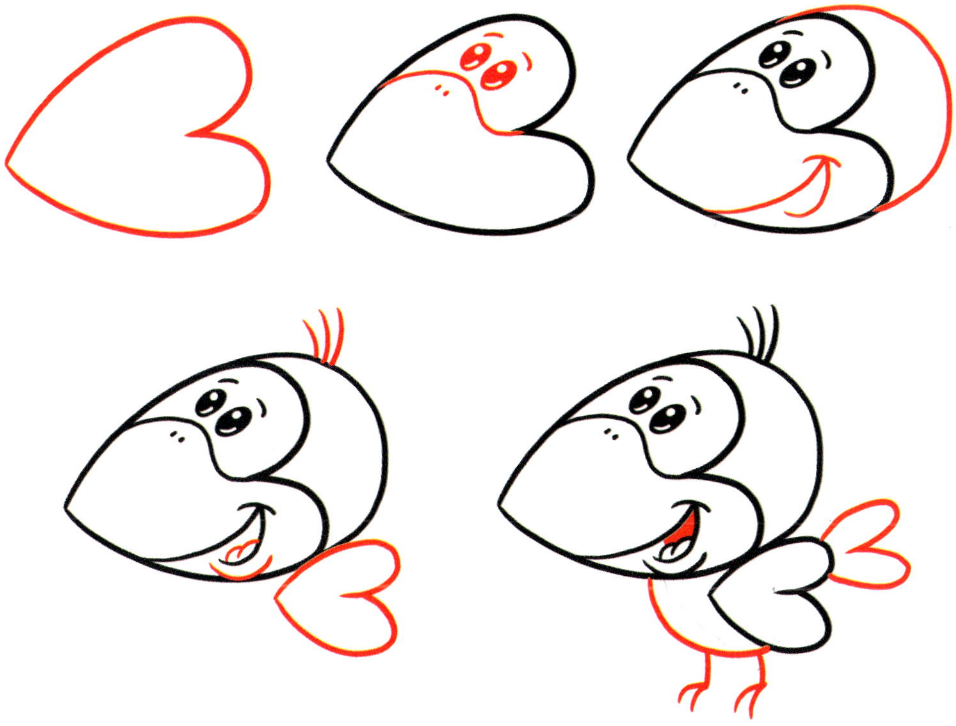

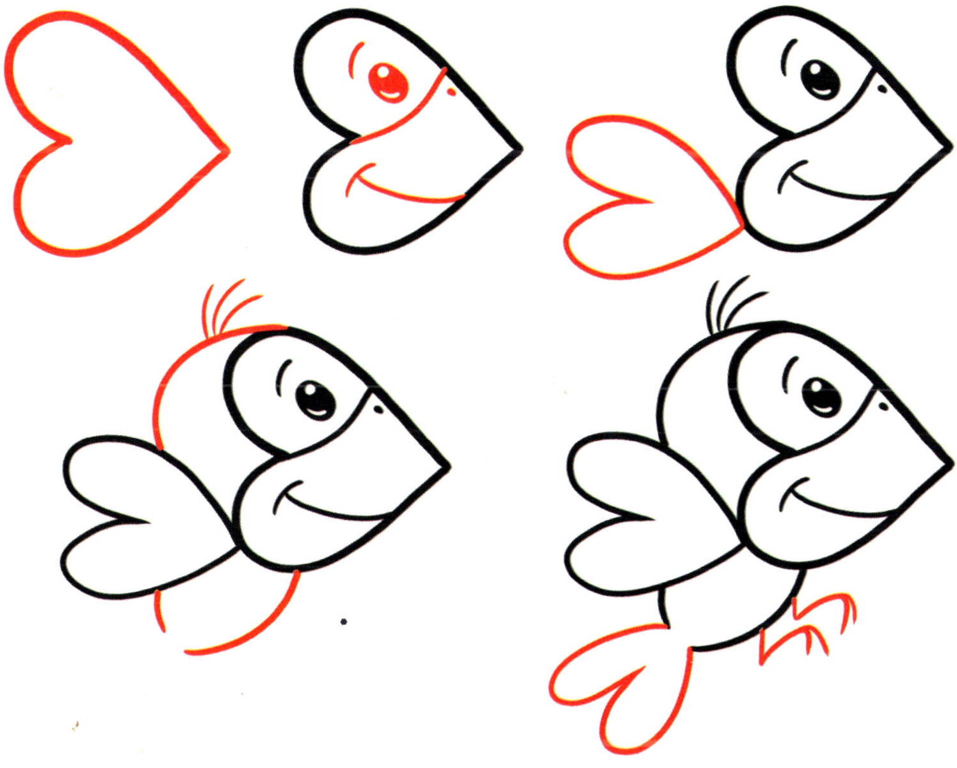

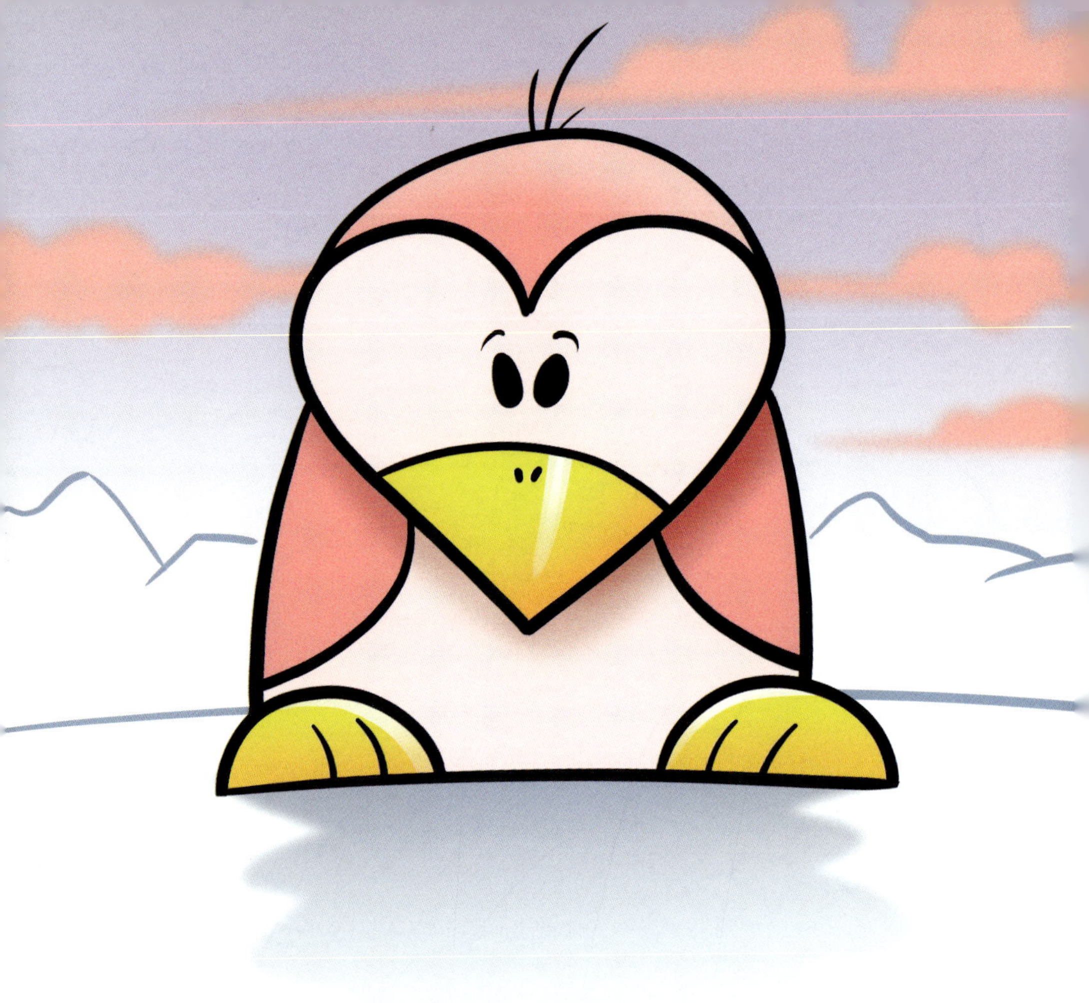

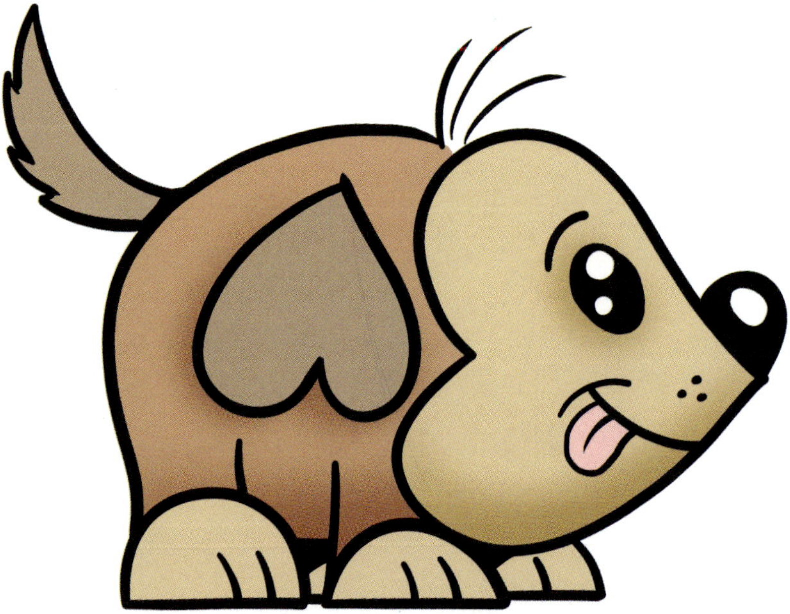

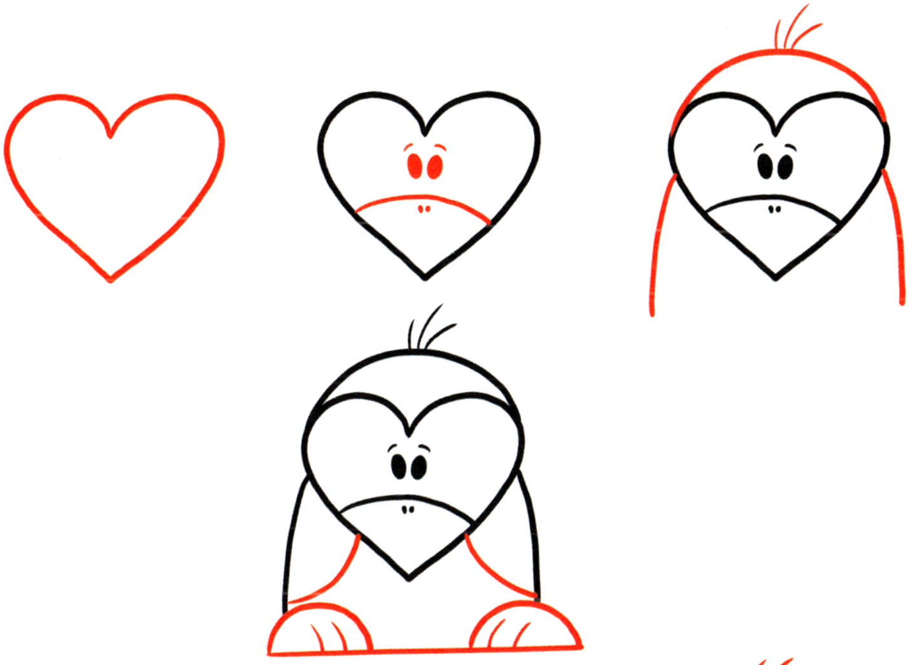

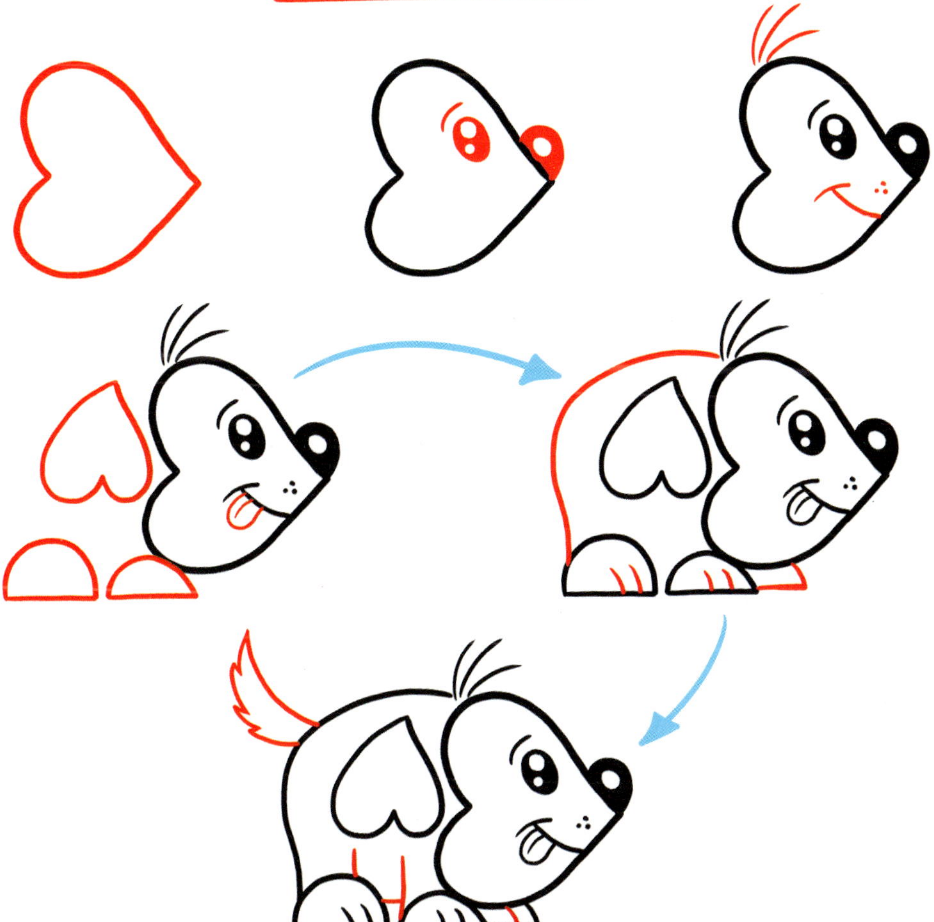

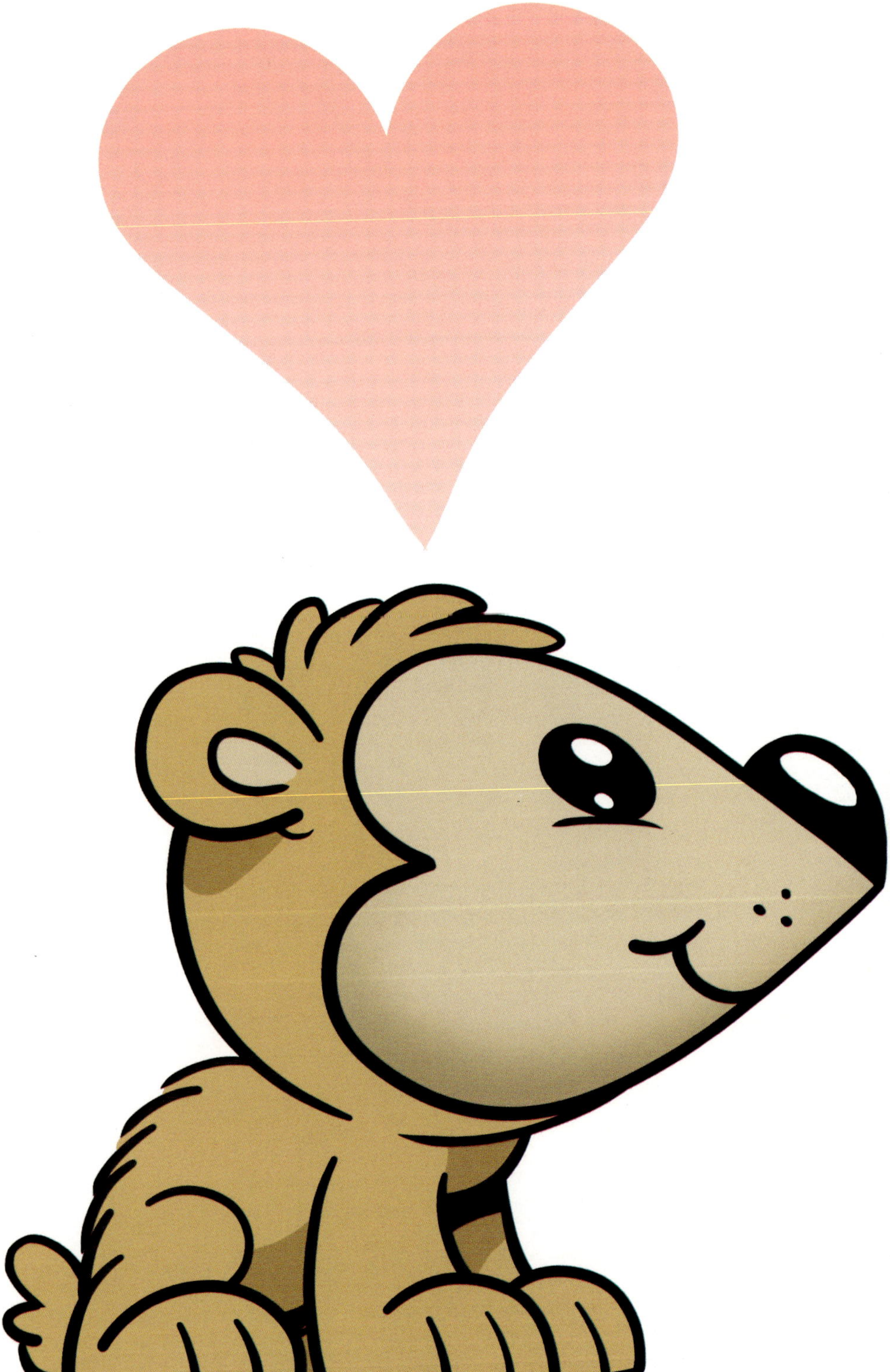

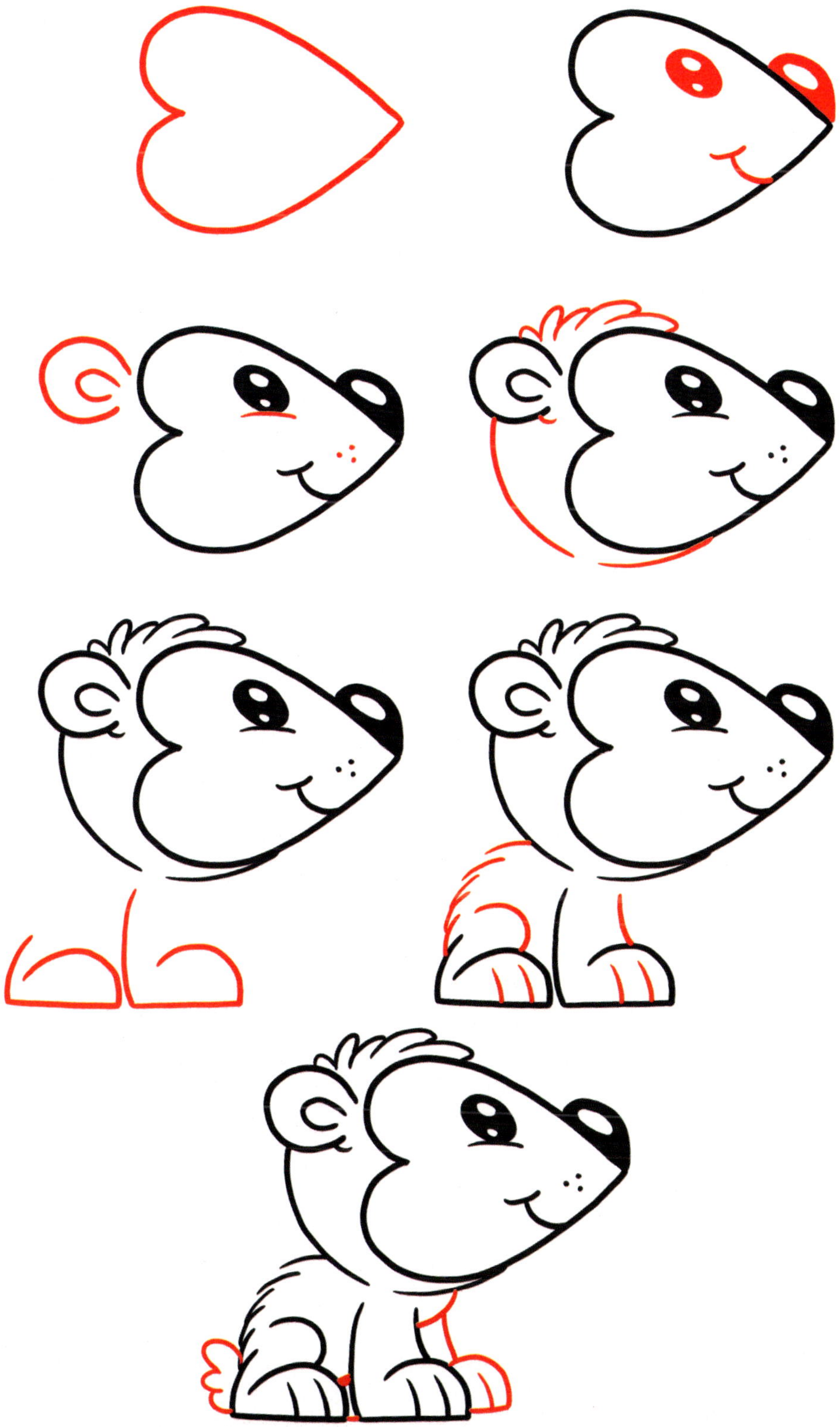

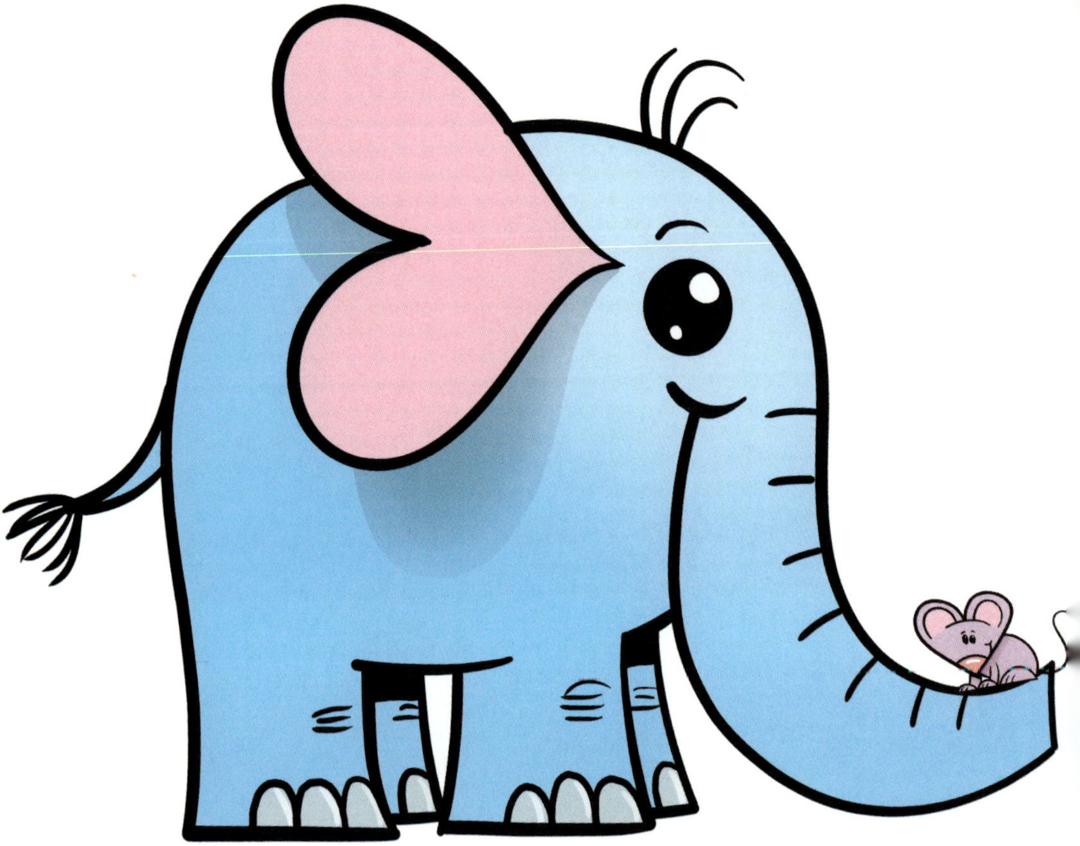

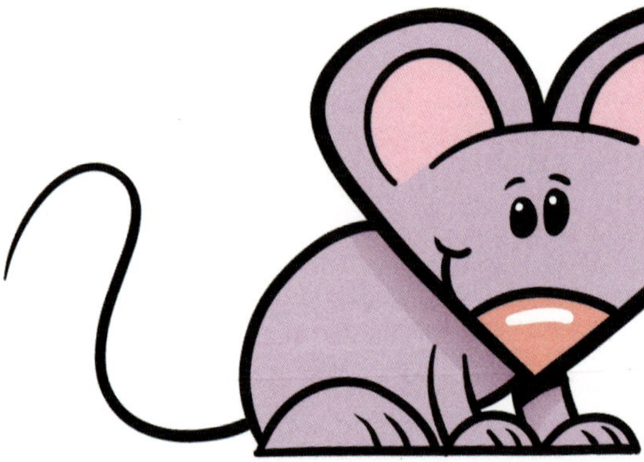

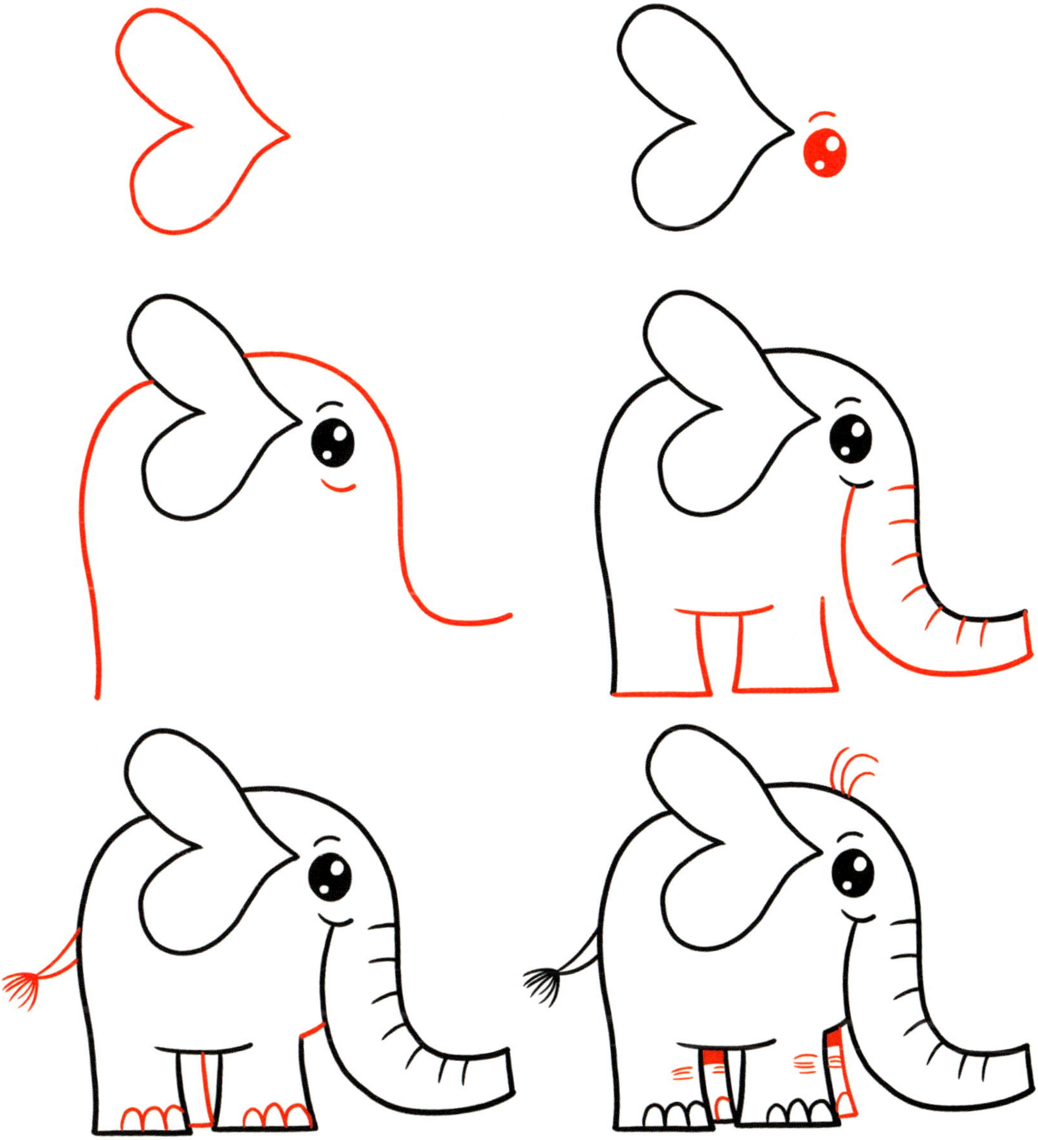

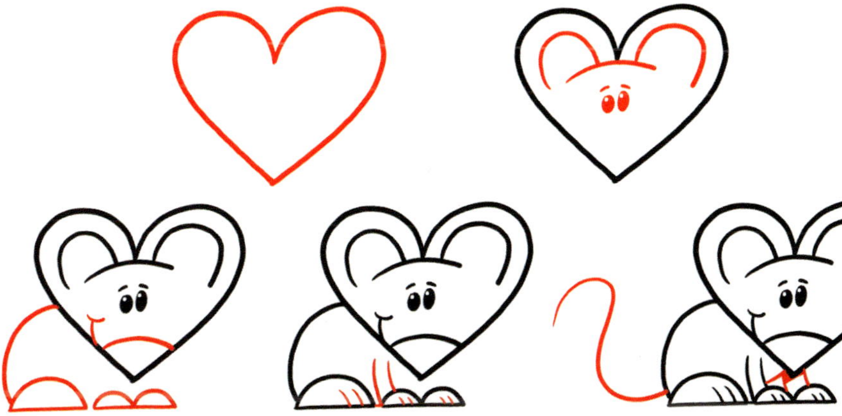

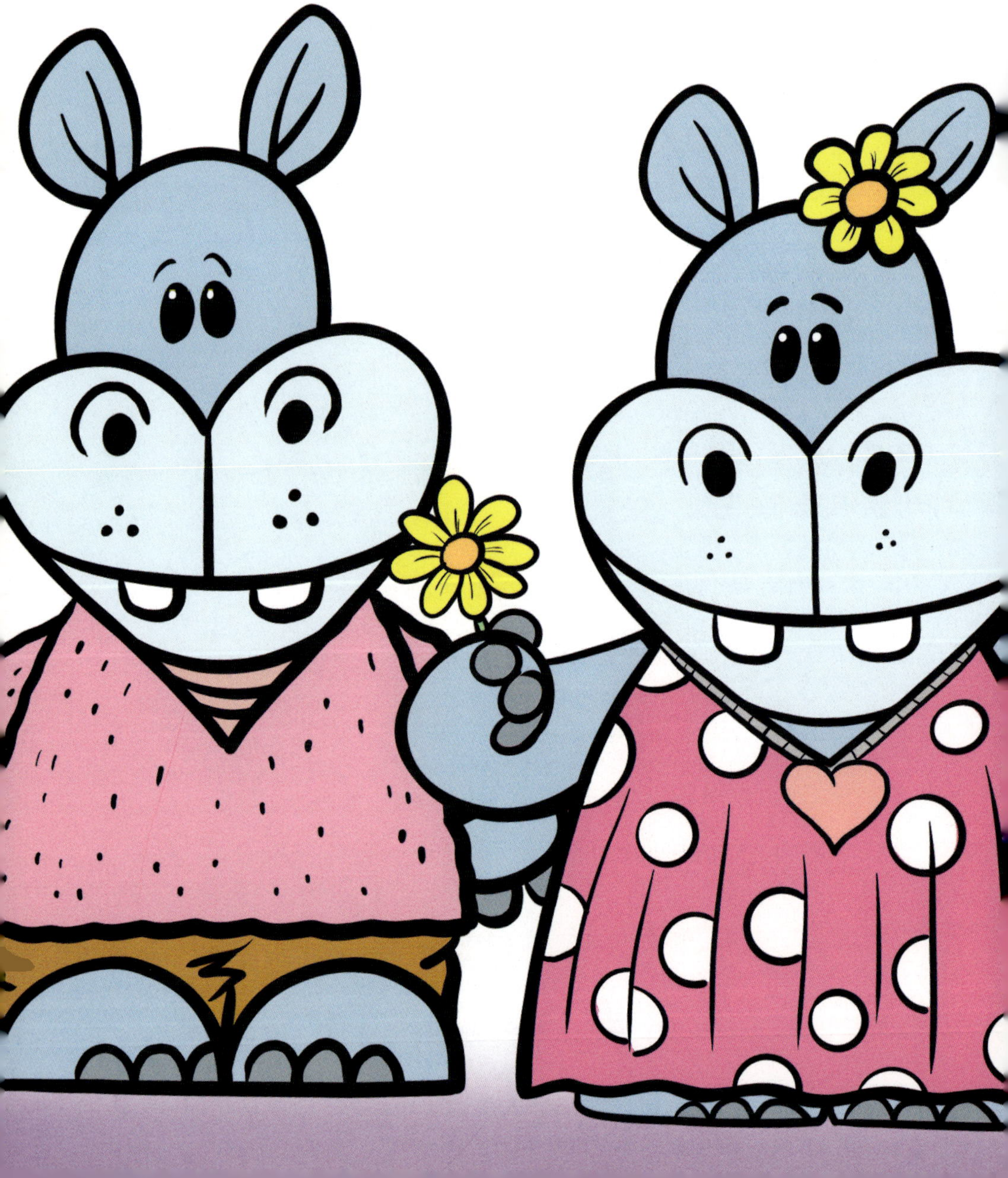

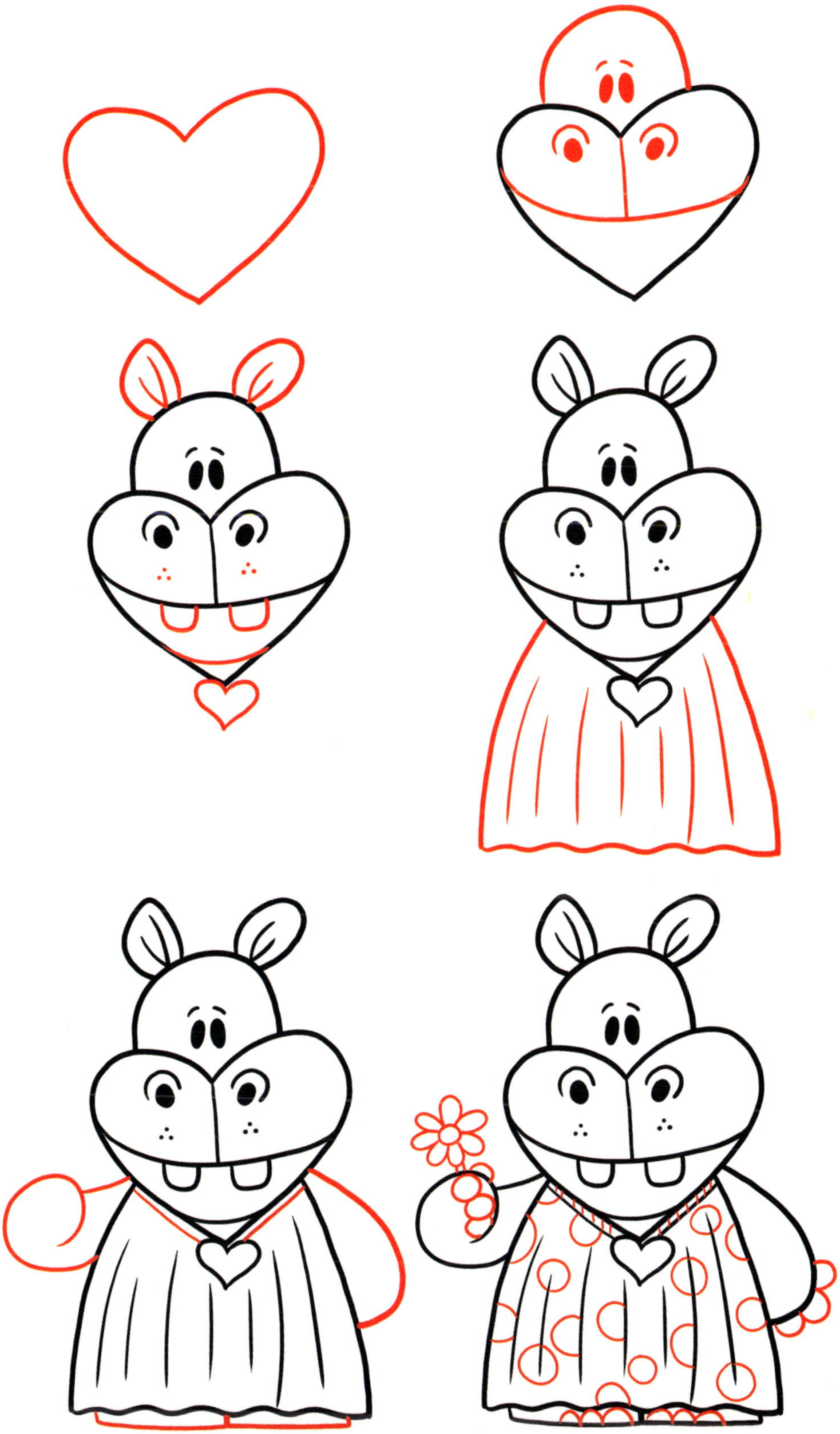

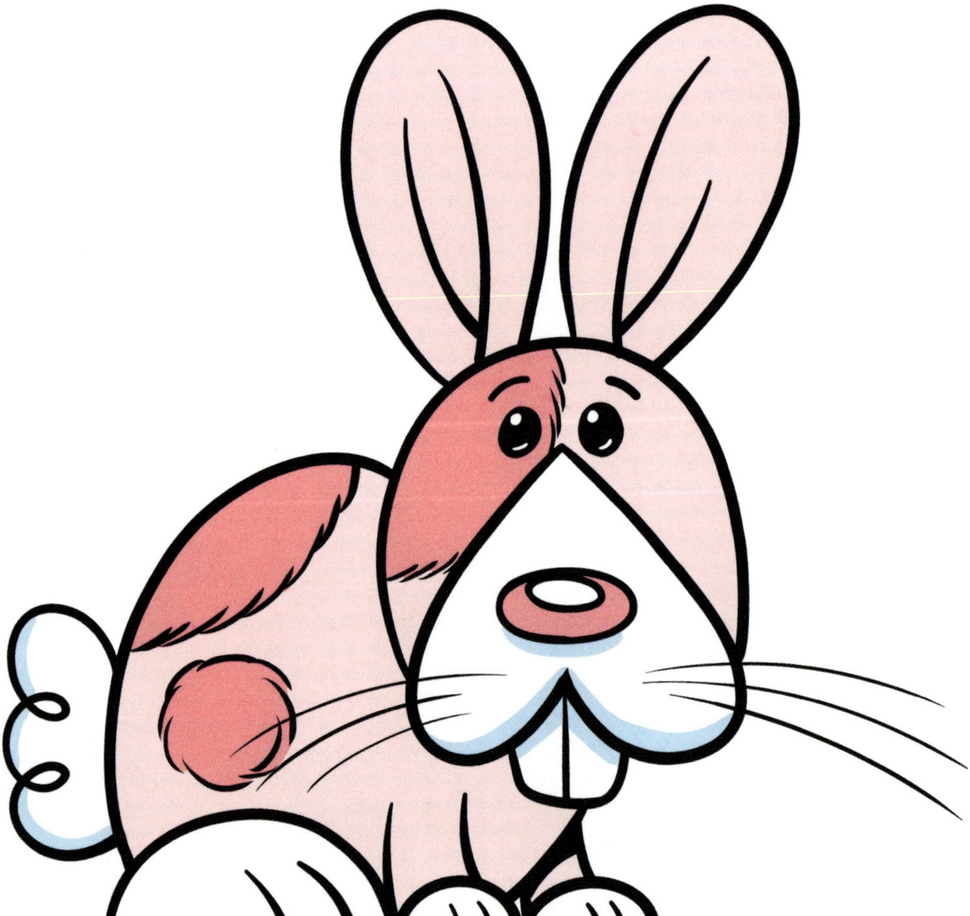

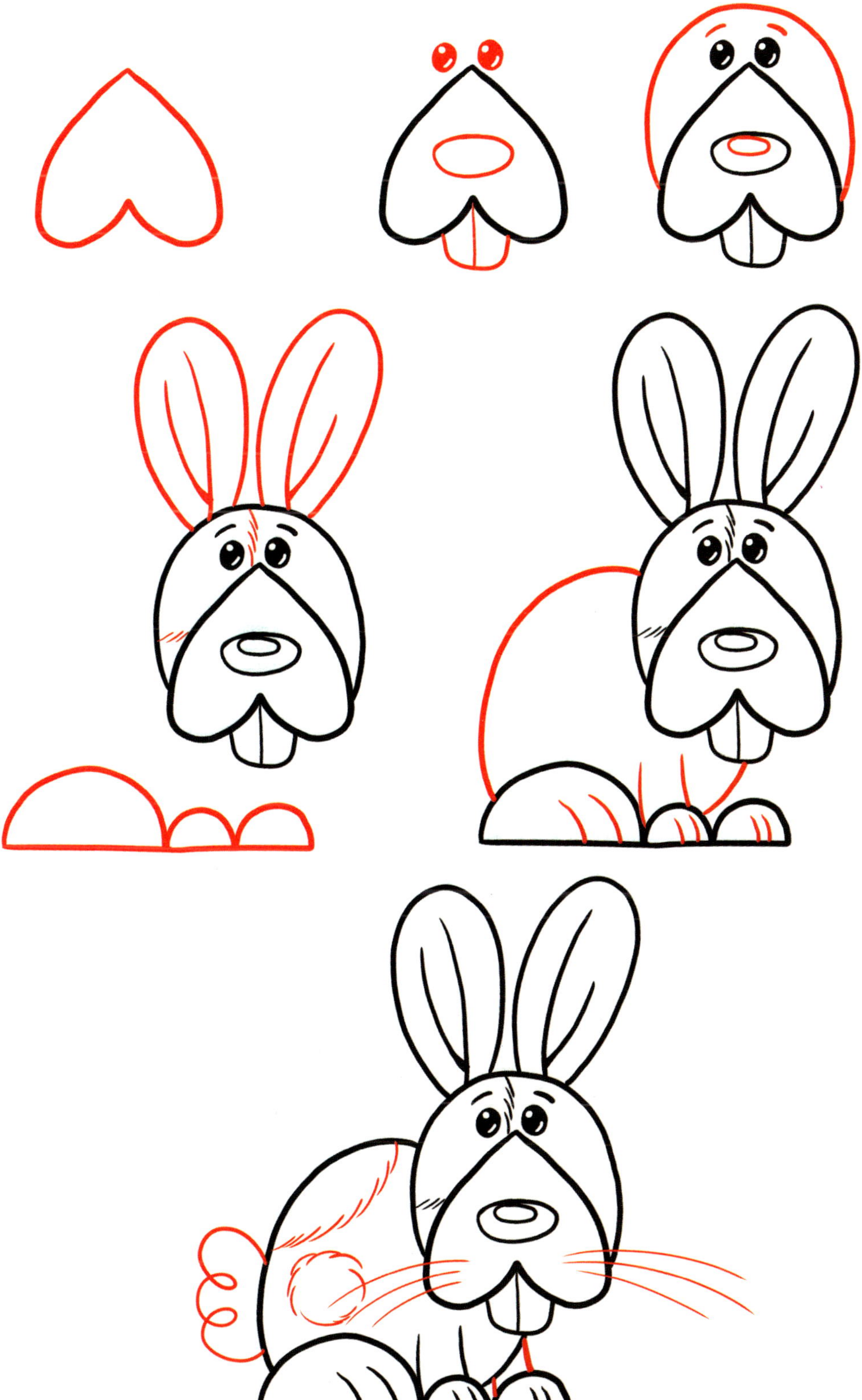

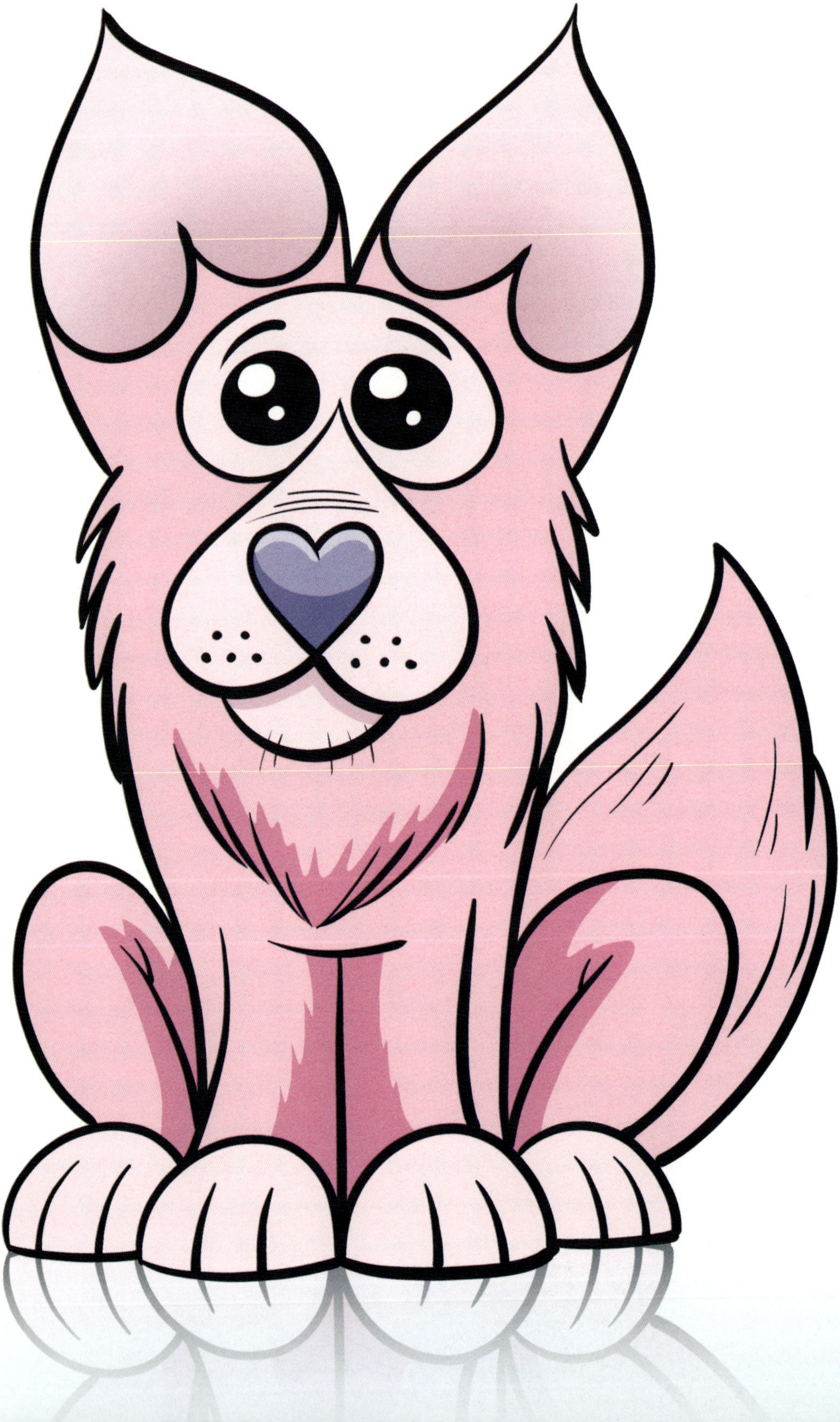

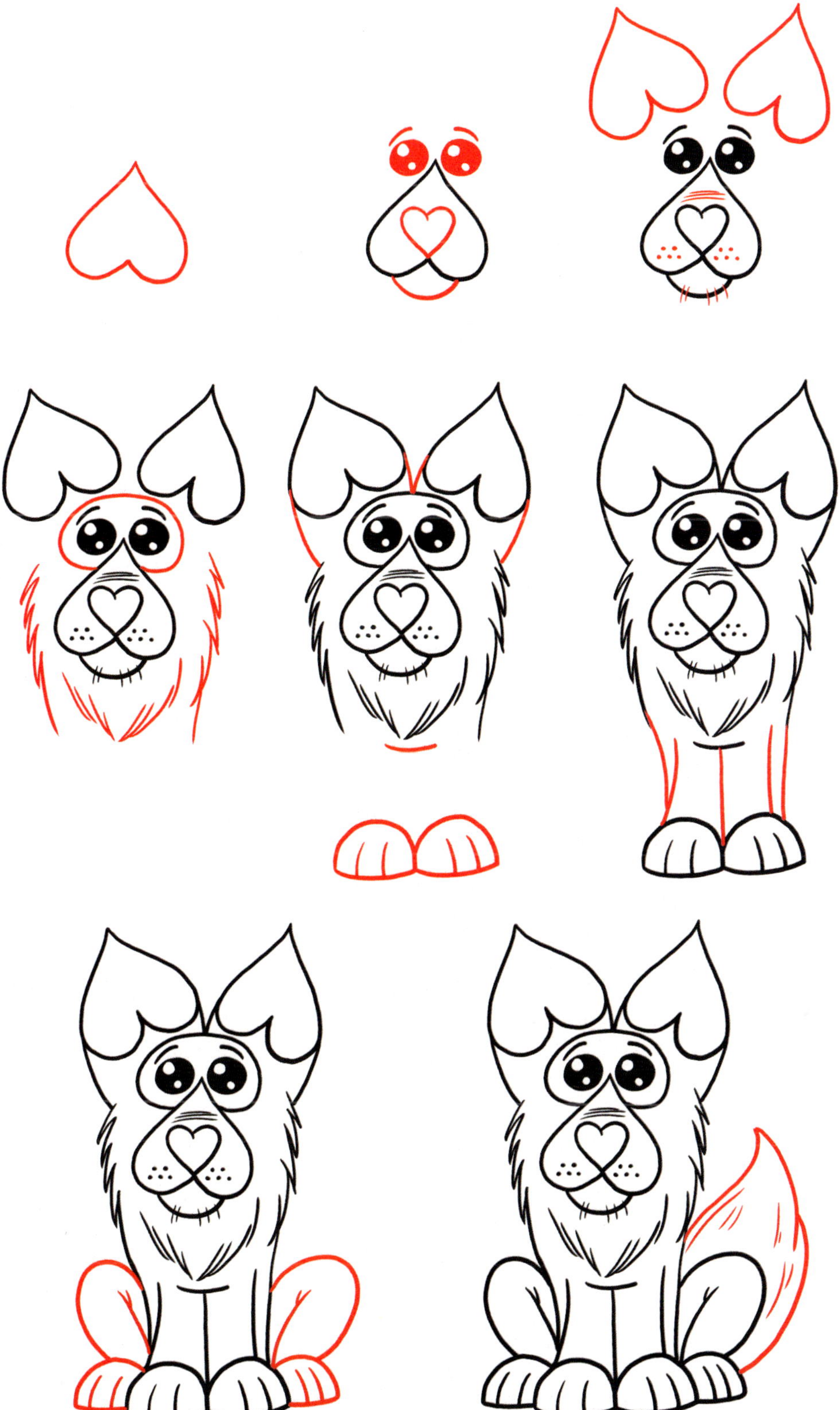

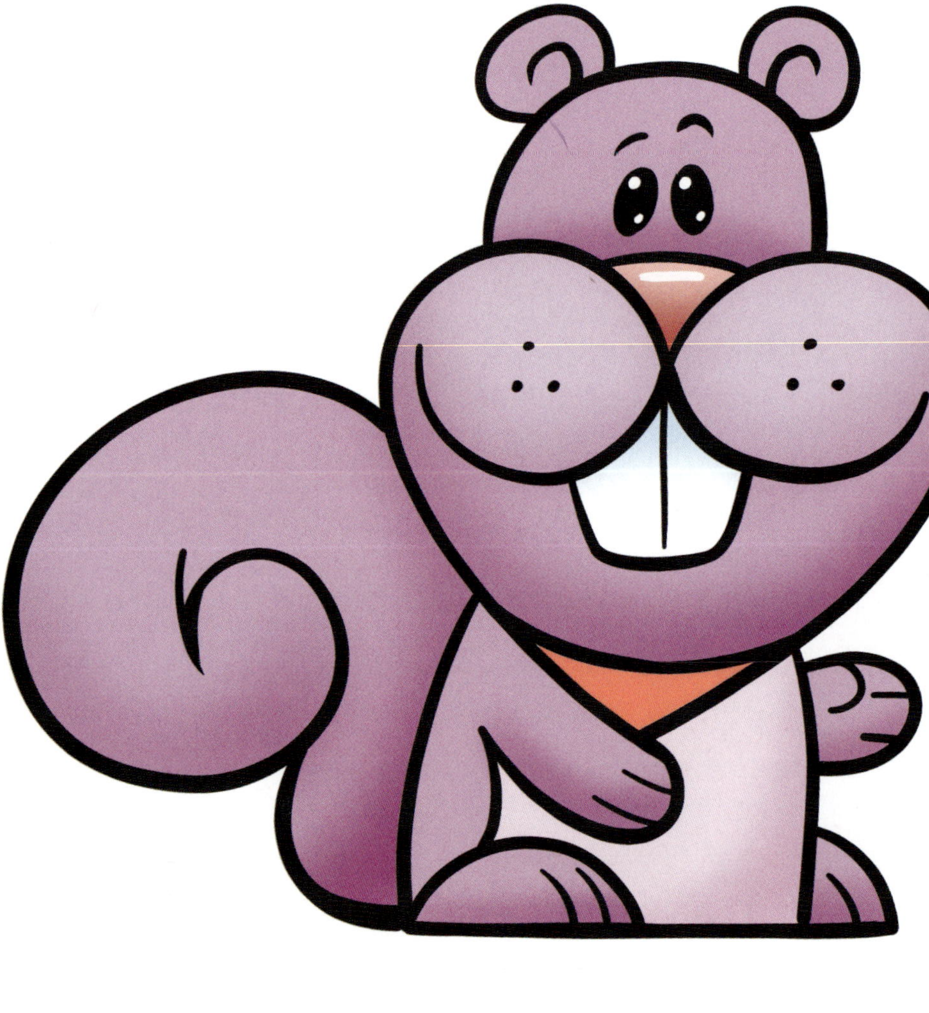

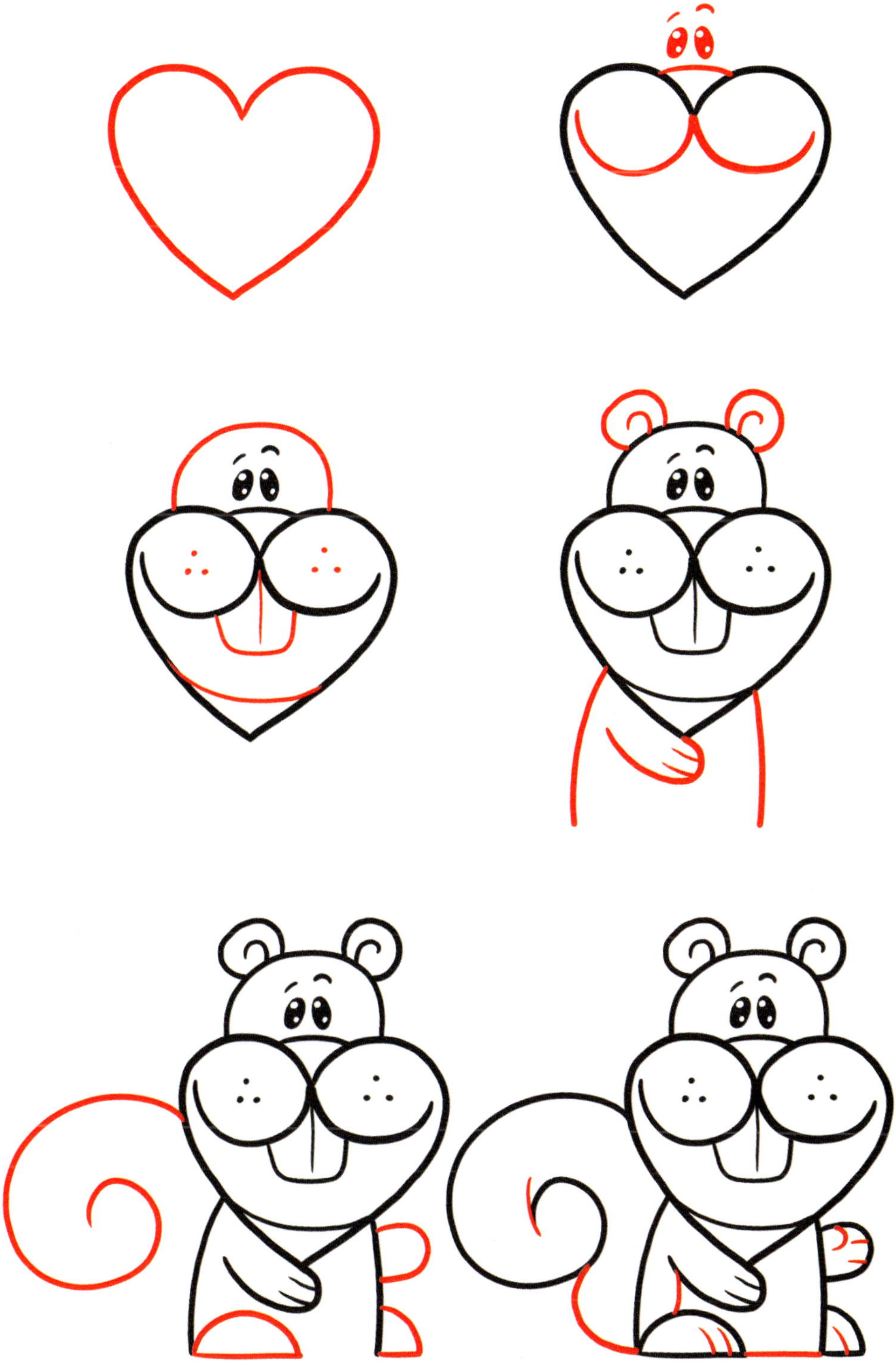

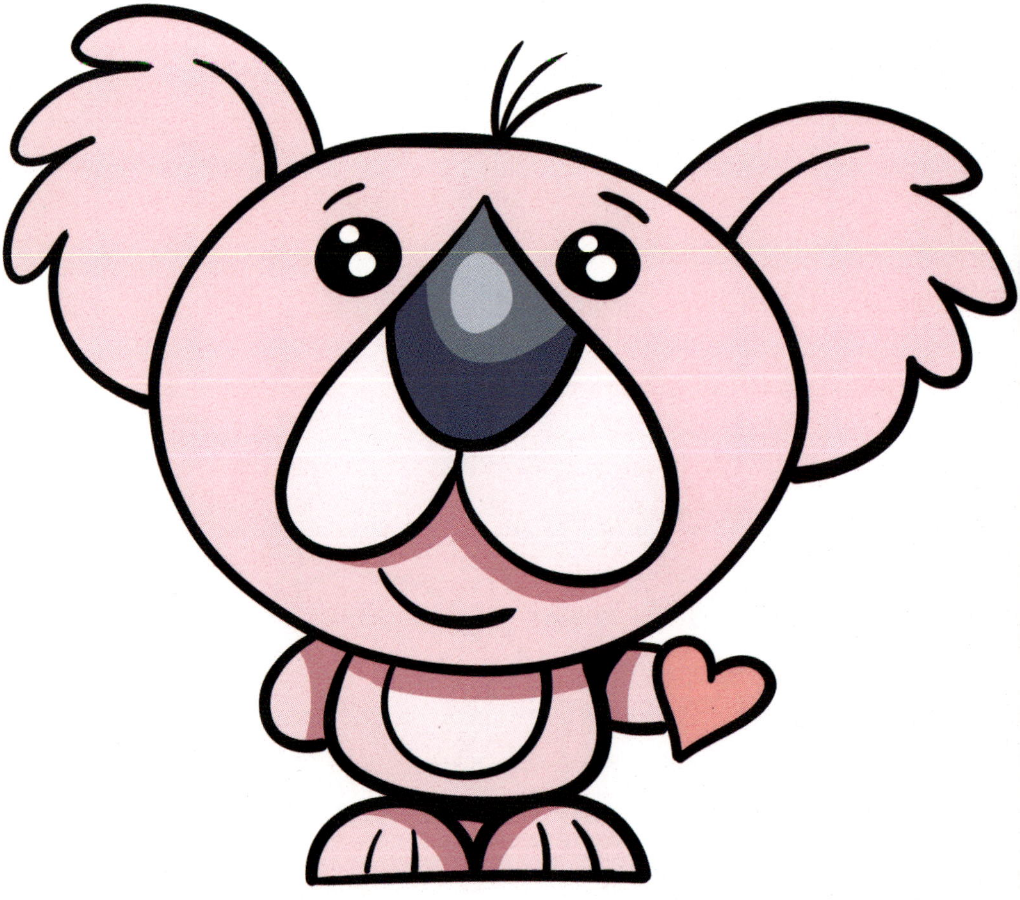

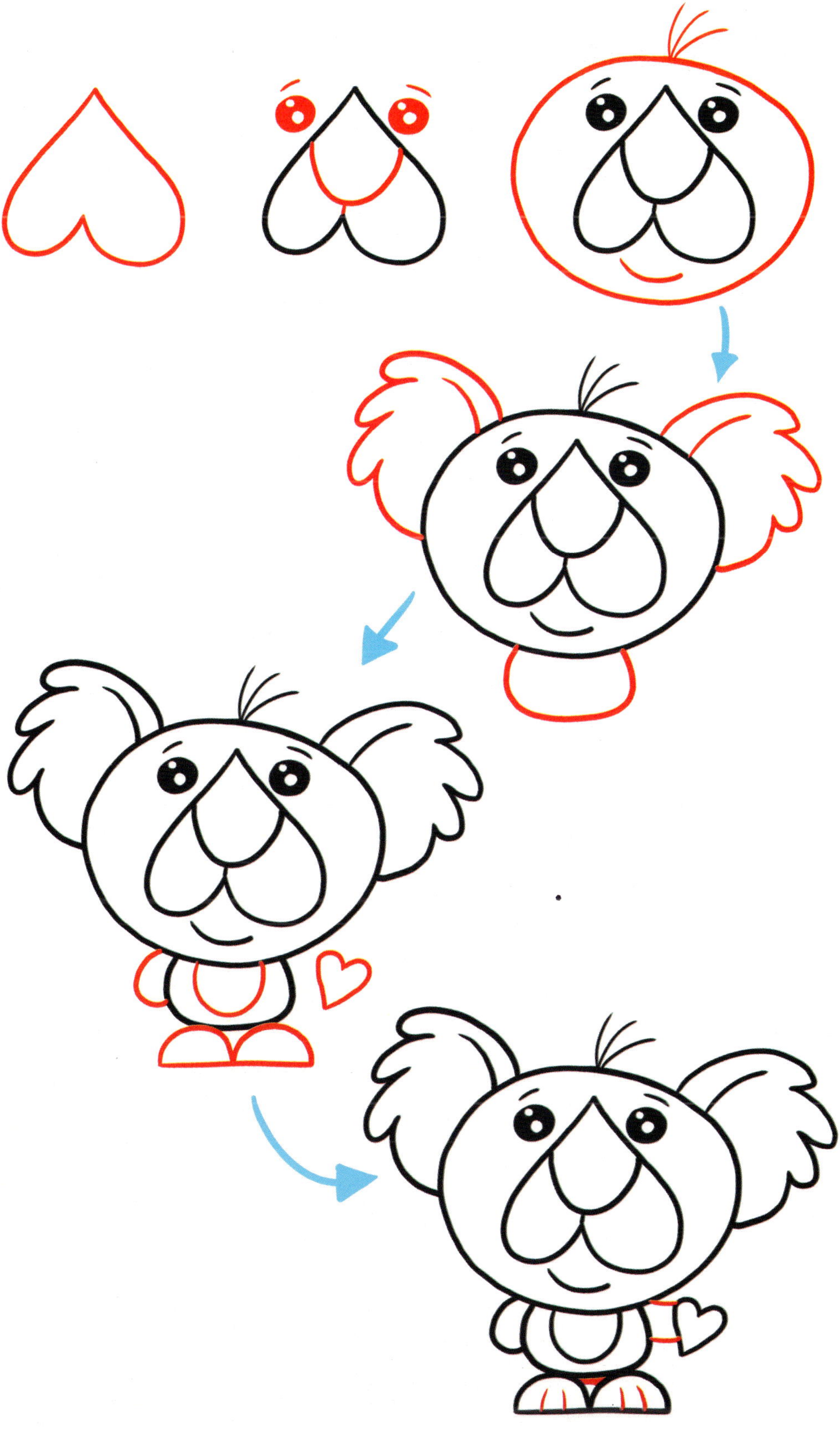

Visit Harptoons.com and watch how-to-draw videos, print off free coloring and activity pages, and create fun crafts. Email your drawings to art@harptoons.com and it might get featured in a Harptoons drawing video. All this and more at the greatest drawing site dedicated to getting young people drawing, creating and imagining.

Follow Harptoons on:

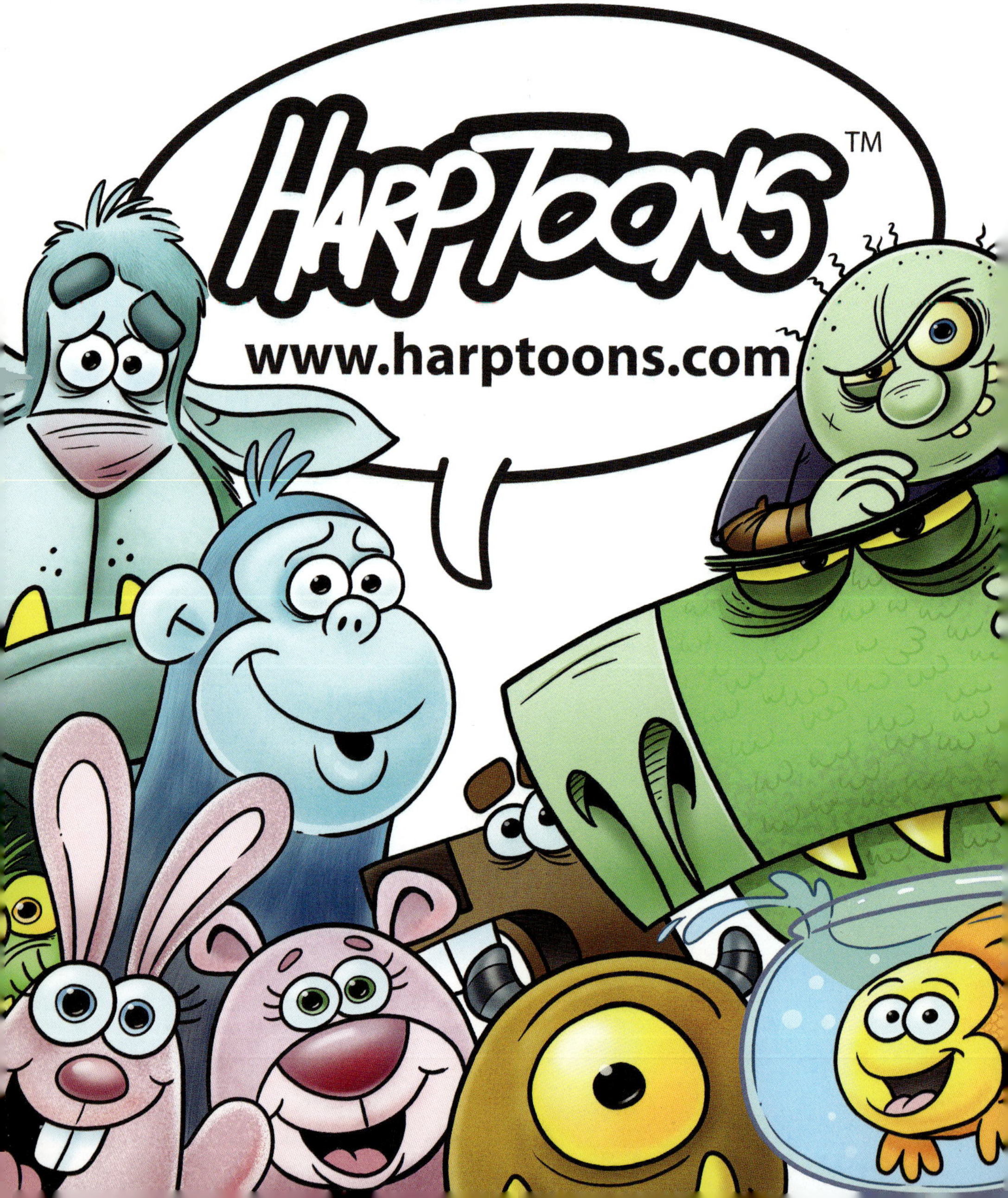